The Misadventures of a Mom Author

VOLUME 1

CAREY HARDISKY

Carey Hardisky

Copyright © 2022 by Carey Hardisky

All rights reserved.

No part of this book may be reproduced in any form or by any electronic or mechanical means, including information storage and retrieval systems, without written permission from the author, except for the use of brief quotations in a book review.

Dedicated to the memory of my dad.

Miss you!

Contents

Acknowledgments vii
About the Author ix

Introduction 1
Saturday, January 2, 2021 4
Tuesday, January 19, 2021 7
February 27, 2021 10
Saturday, March 13, 2021 13
Friday, April 2, 2021 16
Monday, April 12, 2021 19
Friday, May 7, 2021 22
Wednesday, May 12, 2021 25
Sunday, May 16, 2021 28
Monday, May 31, 2021 32
Monday, June 28, 2021 35
Friday, July 9, 2021 3PM 38
Tuesday, July 13, 2021 41
Wednesday, July 14, 2021 44
Wednesday, July 21, 2021 47
Thursday, July 22, 2021 50
Monday, July 26, 2021 53
Saturday, August 7, 2021 56
Saturday, August 14, 2021 60
Tuesday, September 7, 2021 63
Monday, September 20, 2021 66
Thursday, September 30, 2021 69
Wednesday, October 6, 2021 73
Saturday, October 9, 2021 77
Friday, October 15, 2021 80
Sunday, October 17. 2021 84
Friday, October 29, 2021 88
Sunday, October 31, 2021 91
Wednesday, November 10, 2021 94
Friday, November 26, 2021 97

Friday, December 17, 2021	100
Tuesday, January 4, 2022	104
Sunday, January 9, 2022	108
Sunday, January 23, 2022	111
Sunday, January 30, 2022	114
Thursday, February 3, 2022	117
Wednesday, February 16, 2022	120
Monday, February 28, 2022	123
Sunday, March 6, 2022	127
Friday, March 11, 2022	130
Monday, March 21, 2022	133
Friday, March 25, 2022	136
Sunday, March 27, 2022	139
Thursday, March 31, 2022	143
Saturday, April 2, 2022	146
Friday, April 15, 2022	149
Tuesday, April 26, 2022	153
Thursday, May 5, 2022	156
Volume 1 Conclusion	159

Acknowledgments

A special thank you to everyone who made my publishing dream possible. My support network: My parents, sister, husband, little girl, aunts and uncles, Veronica - my sister from another mister, all my friends on Authortube: Charlie, Kat, Glory, Tom, Laura, Megan, Jayce, Haley, Eva, Chandra, Mama Magie, Sako. And so many more.

Special thank you to Charlie who helped design the cover and guiding me through the process and Ray for helping with formatting.

About the Author

Carey Hardisky is the author of the serialized fantasy adventure, *Adventures of Thira*, a short story, *One More Day,* and the upcoming urban fantasy series, *Witches of Coolersville."*

Her love of storytelling started with making up stories with her sister playing dolls; now, she's writing down her stories to share with the world.

When she's not writing or participating in the writing community on YouTube and Twitch, Carey can be found with her family and friends, prepping for the next Renaissance festival, or crocheting something new. Carey lives in a quiet neighborhood near Cleveland, Ohio.

Follow Carey Hardisky on her writing journey or connect with her on social media: https://linktr.ee/CareyHAuthor

Introduction
WRITTEN: THURSDAY, JULY 8, 2021

Why hello there. My name is Carey. I'm a wife, mom, nerd, and I am working to be a published author. Although, I guess if you're reading this, I already am. Woo! But, I've yet to see my fiction published other than a short story I put up on Kindle at the time of this introduction. I am getting there and wanted to document the process. This first volume starts in January 2021 but I've been writing for far longer than that.

I live in a suburb of Cleveland, Ohio with my husband and daughter. We have a small house but it's enough for the 3 of us and the neighborhood is nice and quiet.

I know it's a bit of a cliche about writers but I have loved stories my whole life. Hearing and telling them. I remember falling asleep to my mom reading to me at night. I'd make up wild stories with my dolls. I'd make little stick figure comics. When I got older, I'd get caught scribbling away instead of paying attention in school. I was always coming up with stories. And, sometimes, even finishing them.

In the early 2010s, I was out with a friend and we spent almost the entire time taking turns complaining about our jobs. We both worked retail. We realized we needed to change something. So, we both dedicated to pursuing our creative passions as our career and our way out of the hell hole that is retail. She had a web comic she'd been working on for a while. I had some stories floating around my brain that I decided to try and focus on to publish.

In 2013, I participated in National Novel Writing Month. An event launched every November that challenges you to write a 50,000 word first draft in a month. Why November, I don't know. But, there it is. I spent October outlining and organizing a sort of routine and then jumped in to write. I had a story I was really enjoying. I even did daily videos and shared them on YouTube. At the end of November, I had hit the 50,000 words but the story wasn't done yet. So, I resolved to keep going. I planned on taking December off. Holidays and retail don't mix very well and I knew I'd be mentally and physically exhausted. But, after the new year, I'd pick it up again.

But, that didn't happen. I lost the flash drive I had the story saved on. And, stupid me, it was the only place I had it saved. I didn't find it again for 2 years and by then I was in deep with my other projects. So that book is just known as "The Lost Story."

In April 2014, for Camp NaNoWriMo (which is like regular NaNoWriMo but the rules are slightly more relaxed and they hold it in April and July) I wrote the first draft of what would be book 1 of my Witches of Coolersville series. I started editing it with the intent to publish.

Which I did briefly but then pulled it after a few months. It wasn't my best work. The cover was awful. It wasn't professionally edited or formatted or anything. A couple rounds of critique does not a good book make. So, I pulled it and started fixing it. I'd save my money, write the rest of the series, and do it right.

During that time, I got married to my husband in 2017 and in 2019 we welcomed our daughter into the world.

A few things to note as you continue reading. For the sake of privacy, I will be using nicknames for people when I mention them. When I mention Hubby, he's Hubby or Husband. When I mention my kiddo, she's Peanut.

So, that's all for this part of the tale. Now travel back with me to the early days of 2021 and come along on the journey. Happy reading.

Saturday, January 2, 2021

Well, here we go. It is the start of a new year and my rewrite continues. I, by some miracle, managed to rewrite book 1 before the holidays and am finishing my rewrite of book 2. My plan is to outline and first draft as much of the series as I can this year, then go back to the beginning, flesh it out, clean it up, and work on the steps toward publishing. During this time, I will be paying down debt, working on researching so I am ready for the business aspect, building my platform, all while raising a high energy toddler and working a part time job in the middle of a pandemic.

(If anyone reads this 100 years from now, look up all the things that happened in this time period. I'm sure it will be in your history books)

Some background about me: My name is Carey. I am (at the time of this entry) 36 years old. I have a part time job as a front desk receptionist at a nursing home. I'm married to a wonderful man and we have a beautiful little girl who will be 2 this May. Mom life keeps me running until I think I am about to fall over. On top of just being an energetic toddler, she has physical and occupational therapy appointments each once a week. I work every other weekend and some Fridays at my job. Hubby works as a draftsman at a small architecture firm in Cleveland.

I had the day off today. So, I spent the day shut away in the office trying to declutter the place. It's... well, it looks like a tornado blew through so I am doing what I can. It is exhausting work. Fortunately, Hubby was cool about being Toddler Control today. We have a pretty good routine where, since I have most days of the week, he takes over and lets me work on evenings and non-other job weekends. And Peanut loves it. She is totally a Daddy's girl and it is adorable. He comes home and she crawls as fast as her little arms and legs will go. It is so stinking funny.

I can't believe she is almost 20 months now. Where did the time go? I already know I will be one of those moms that cries at every milestone. I also think this work is important to show her that you can achieve your dreams with enough hard work. It may be a long road with a lot of bumps. But, when you have support and determination, you can move mountains.

Wow, that sounds so cheesy. But, it is true. Nothing is handed to you. No fairy godmother hands you a publishing contract or a gig with an art gallery or whatever. I will probably be completely gray by the time I publish in 3 years but it will be a party! I turn 40 that year! Book launch and cake! Peanut also will be in kindergarten by then so I should have more time to focus on writing and business management.

In the meantime, I can study the industry and build my platform. I started a new thing this year. I plan on doing a monthly vlog as a further look "behind the pages." The series has the same title as this journal. I don't think I'll go into as much detail on video as I will in writing. Otherwise I would have a ton of editing to do to make sure each video isn't five hours long. It is also more convenient to write a journal entry in the evening rather than hauling my camera everywhere and eating through batteries. The video series is more of a fun project just to have a little content on my YouTube channel.

Here's to a new year. Dear God, let it be better than the last one.

Tuesday, January 19, 2021

So, the past two days were toast for me. I went up to work on Sunday to get my second half of the vaccine for this virus that has been plaguing the world. I had a bit of a headache that day but Peanut was being particularly loud and sounding like a Velociraptor, as toddlers tend to do. So, that could have been the contributor to said headache. Woke up next day, felt fine and went about the day.

Until, that is, I put Peanut down for her nap.

Then, it was like a switch flipped. Oh my gosh, it was awful. I had no energy at all so I went and took a 3 hour nap myself. When I woke up, I felt like I had been run over by a truck. Full body aches and chills. I forced myself to make dinner and then told Hubby he was on his own the rest of the night. It wasn't anything that I couldn't sleep off so that was good. My side effects were on the mild end, I suppose. But, it beats the condition it protects against so there's that. I'll take an afternoon of needing to sleep over the alternative. And, honestly, I needed the sleep because I've had to pull a couple all-nighters with Peanut. So, this did me some good in more ways than one.

Today was much better, though. Took Peanut to her therapy session, came back, she went down for her nap nearly right away, and then I went to work on writing. I made some final touches to book 2 and then started to outline book 3. I'm a little ahead of schedule so that's great. My plan is to have up to book 9 or 10 outlined and with a first draft by the end of the year. I'm pretty sure I can do it. I don't know how many books there will be but I like a long series. My writing style for this is very episodic. There is an overall antagonist with a "baddy of the week." At least, for the first few books. I have some ideas in the future that will change things up in the format but it's going to be great. If I ever get my books adapted, one book could be at least part of a season.

If I ever did an adaptation in another form of media, I'd probably do an audio drama. That would be the audiobook. I got the idea while I was binge listening to my friend Sarah's podcast. It's a science fiction radio drama and it is AWESOME! So, I started thinking about my audio drama and the books aren't even done yet!

Tomorrow I don't know how much writing I'll do. We're having a watch party for the Inauguration with my mom and sister. We're all meeting on Skype or Google Meet or something like that to watch together. I'll probably enjoy some wine later as well because why not? I don't identify with any particular party. I think there are a lot of flaws in the system and people need to do better at coming together to work it out for the better of all. But, I have rarely missed watching an Inauguration ceremony in my adult life regardless of who won. I like to pay attention to historical events, that's all. When my grandkids come to me for a family history interview or if they're writing my biography, I want to be prepared, ha.

Lots of time left in the week to get writing done.

February 27, 2021

GUYS! I just finished an interview with the cast of an audio drama on my YouTube channel and it was AMAZING! I discovered this Power Rangers fan drama podcast and loved it so much that I sent the creator an email. Shot in the dark, I asked if he'd like to come on my little channel and do an interview with a few cast members and he said yes! I couldn't believe it!

It took some time to plan because everyone was in different timezones. The creator is in England. One of the cast members is Australian I think? And the rest who were available were from all over the States. We talked about their version of the show and geeked out about the Power Rangers, growing up watching it, and it was just so cool. I was nervous. I'd never had that many people guest on my channel before but I managed to get the questions in a way that everyone could take part.

I also put on a full face of makeup. I never do that anymore. With all the mask mandates, there's no point in doing a whole face of makeup only to have it rubbed off from the nose down. If I wear makeup to work, it's eyeshadow only. So, since this was an occasion, I had to go all out. And, I brought out some off my geekery. I have the pink and green ranger action figures that I found at an old toy store. They have a spot on top of my desk now. I would love to find the full set someday.

I watched the Mighty Morphin Power Rangers in the early 90s. It was a huge part of my childhood. Yes, it's cheesy as heck and there are some things where you look back and think, "mmm, would this be problematic now?" But, even now, it's a little bit of fun. I like my 90s cheese. I've even met one of the actors at a comic convention. I've met Jason David Frank who played Tommy on the series, and returned in following versions of the show. He is one of the most genuine and cool people I've ever met. He will geek out about the fandom right along with you and it is so fun.

In writing news, still making my way through book 3. Finishing up some things while also getting a jump on book 4. That should be pretty easy to outline and then write. I'm getting these holiday story ideas that have been different but fun. Book 3 takes place surrounding Halloween. Book 4 is around Christmas. As my main cast are mostly witches, I like figuring out how they would celebrate these holidays. Nobody really has one faith that they follow. Although, Gran does attend a local Catholic Church, she's not a strict practitioner. She goes because she likes the community there and it's where her husband attended. It was fun coming up with the memorial ritual in book 3. I kind of blended All Souls Day with other rituals and traditions from various sources to make my own concoction. I still need to flesh out some details but I was getting a little choked up as I wrote it. I even pulled up an old poem of mine for my main character to recite. I don't normally write poetry. It was an assignment for a college English class and I had just lost my one grandmother.

My goal is to finish book 4 first draft in March and book 5 outline in April. I think I have an idea of what to write. I know the tie-ins from the previous books and I want to feature a person I've only shown glimpses of so far. Here's hoping this isn't a repeat of book 3 where I'm spending way too much time trying to figure things out.

Saturday, March 13, 2021

Today was a very productive day. It was the Worldwide Write-a-Thon on YouTube so I knocked out a couple hours. Made up for all the stuff I did not do over the course of the week. I wrote some at work last night so that helped, too. But, I mostly finished my outline of book 4. I say mostly as there are many parts in double parentheses that are ((things happen here with a lot of details I need to flesh out.)) Mostly in the last couple chapters when it gets very magic heavy. It happened in the two previous books, too.

This book was easy to outline compared to book 3. That was so hard to nail down! I tried on and off for almost 4 years. It was partly because I was trying from another character point of view. And partly was everything that went on in the past 4 years. Marriage, job changes, kids, pandemic. Yeah, I'll be glad for the day we don't have to talk about THAT anymore. Also, I came to some other realizations that will involve more from-the-start major changes. But, I'll have to worry about that when I get to that point. I did write it down so that is a start. I have notebooks for each book and then a sort of catch all book for overall notes. Because I am a sleep-deprived, scatter-brained mess of a human being and I forget things if they're not written in a notebook or on my phone.

I don't mind that I was slightly behind on my goal though. The weather was perfect this week so I had to take Peanut to enjoy it. Took her to the park and we walked and went on the swings. Even took one day and spent it at Cleveland Zoo, thanks to their free Mondays for county residents. It was so nice, even if it was short-lived. Spring in the Great Lakes region is all 4 seasons in the same week. Fun!

Also today, I took my dad to church so he could see everyone after his illness. On the way back, we talked about how he wants to write his memoirs. But, he doesn't know where to start. I think I am going to give him some of my spare notebooks so he can start brainstorming what he wants to share and we will go from there. I shared on one of the writing groups I'm on that this is going to be a project we're going to try and work on together and they were great and suggested all kinds of resources to help. I think, for a Father's Day gift, I'm going to get him a few of the recommended books. I don't know if he would want to publish it. If nothing else, we can get it bound and pass it to the grandbabies so they have stories and lessons from their Papa. It would be cool if he published it, though. I think he has a lot of things he could share from his varied experiences that people can benefit from.

When I got back home, I chatted online with some friends. I told them about my progress so far. I'm excited to keep moving forward in this series. Book 4 will be a lot of fun to write. I've had ideas for that for a while. I know it'll take place at Christmas. I know supernatural and fantastical shenanigans will ensue, possibly having to do with a full moon. I want there to be a cult that worships a particular creature. And, that's all I can share. But, it's going to be fun to write and I can't wait to dive in.

My brain is fried and it's time change tonight so I need to sleep.

Friday, April 2, 2021

I had to dedicate today to office declutter and laundry. Not done with either yet but I made a large dent. I have a perhaps unconventional and slightly inefficient method but it works for me. I put everything in a box or bin just to make space, throwing things out as I go. And then I sort what is in each box. Doing a little at a time eases the overwhelm and I will actually accomplish something and avoid the heart palpitations that come with the total mess. I am hoping next week I will have made room to bring the exercise bike from the basement. I thought about the living room again but I can't risk Peanut getting her fingers pinched. With the nicer weather, I want to exercise more and that should help my back. I marked a bunch of workout videos to get me started.

I finished the draft of book 4 and am starting trying to outline book 5. A lot of unknowns for this one. I know what needs to be carried over from previous books, especially 4. A LOT happens in book 4. But, as for the big picture tale, I don't know yet. But, I am ahead of schedule. Technically don't have to finish the outline until the end of May. I thought about shifting the goal deadlines but also life happens and I may need that extra time. It's happened before. I give myself a self-imposed deadline and then it all blows up.

I don't think I'll get much writing done this weekend. Unless I try to do something at work. It's Easter weekend. Tomorrow, we're going to dinner at my in-laws when I get done with work. And, Sunday we're going to my parents. I have 2 really cute dresses for Peanut to wear. Thank goodness for hand-me-downs. I think about 90% of her wardrobe is handed down from Bestie's kids. And, the first year, it helped because she grew so much so fast! I don't think she got to wear a majority of what was in her closet. Granted, she's still little for almost 2. But, compared to where she started, she's huge. And, I swear she's pure muscle. And she burns every calorie she takes in. But, her pediatrician isn't worried. As long as she's growing, she is where she needs to be.

Easter will be fun, though. The weather will be beautiful. Sunshine, warm, springtime perfection as it should be. It will be good to see family for a special occasion. Won't be able to see my sister. She's still being cautious until all the adults get their vaccines. So, maybe in May when Peanut and her son have birthdays. I'm disappointed but I understand being cautious. And, as things progress this summer, we'll have more chances to see each other and, hopefully, return to some form of normal. Mom definitely wants us all to go to the zoo together. I did warn her, though, I'll probably have to sit at every bench because my back is messed up from a car accident a couple years ago and I can walk only so much before I need to rest for a few minutes. Another reason I need to get the bike in my office. And, I'm going to take Peanut for more walks in our neighborhood to build up my strength again.

Hoping that this week I can make more progress on this outline. I did some brainstorming and wrote down the carried over plot threads. But, beyond that, I'm stuck. Maybe I'll look over some prompts. That usually seems to help me.

Monday, April 12, 2021

This series is making me insane. I am getting all these new ideas that involve changes from the start but I need to move on! On the plus side, I haven't published so when these changes need to be made, I can do it. Part of the reason I am doing this drafting thing. Continuity is important. I come up with an idea and I write it down for when I go back to edit. I can better make sure I can work any massive changes through the whole series.

I am trying to nail down book 5. I did some brainstorm and started a timeline. I'm working on all the tie-in threads but need a "Monster of the week." I need some magical shenanigans to happen. Not just drama.

I also made notes of my big changes that must be made series-wide. I am changing the race of a character, another's sexuality, I decided one person isn't sweary enough. I also realized that one character had her final child in her 50s. While not impossible, it can be incredibly difficult. But, that can be handwaved "because magic" I think. It is a common trope that magical people (wizards, witches, etc) have a longer lifespan than your average human. I think in Harry Potter, Dumbledore was well over 100 years old.

I do have until the end of May to outline according to my goals. Not changing my deadlines if I finish early on a project. Then I have some added flexibility when I have trouble with ideas or when life is a dick. If the past 2 years have taught me anything, it's build in that "just in case" buffer into any of my tasks.

In a hope to get some ideas, I made some character boards on a story planning app I heard about from another writer I follow on YouTube. I found some art and some photos of actors to stand in as character inspiration. When I was writing book 4 last month, I could not get John Barrowman out of my head when I wrote one character. This character is good at changing his accent whenever he wants. And, I thought it would be a fantastic idea if I were able to cast John Barrowman to voice this character whenever I do my audio drama version. It's a dream for sure. I don't know what I'd have to pay to hire him but it's probably out of my price range.

And, today was a prime example why I needed that extra time. Nothing got done. I needed a mindless day. Watch TV and just be a bum. In my defense, Peanut got up at 5 this morning screaming so my brain refused to function. This week won't be nearly as busy as last week so I will have more time to write. Might focus on declutter on Friday. Then I can get the exercise bike in the office. I know I was talking about this for months now but I'll get it in the office before summer.

I'm hoping to get some work done this evening when Hubby comes home. We'll have dinner and then I'll go to my office to write... or try to write. A few writers host livestreams on

YouTube where people come together to write and chat. They set a timer for, say, 20 minutes and everyone has to write as much as they can before time is up. It helps with focused productivity. At least it works for me. And then, there is chatting for a few minutes in between. Everyone shares their progress, some people share quotes of what they wrote. There's one person I see frequently who writes Iron Man fanfiction. L, a horror writer, shares these beautifully vivid and creepy descriptions and I can't wait to read her work! And, I'm not even much into horror. I know she's trying to get into some anthologies with her short stories.

Time to go. Peanut has therapy tomorrow.

Friday, May 7, 2021

So this week... happened. I mean, it was a lot of fun for the most part. We celebrated Peanut's birthday. My sweet baby girl is 2 years old! I tried a new recipe for dinner when my in-laws came over. I made sloppy joes and chip fries which was a huge hit. I got... some writing done but nowhere near the amount I wanted to this week. I had a few appointments for Peanut. She had Speech therapy and we saw a sleep medicine doctor to make sure she's okay because sometimes she doesn't want to sleep. And, she didn't want to nap. So, Mom Life took priority.

Tomorrow, I have to get some bloodwork done for an appointment of my own and then I am shutting myself away in my office to either write or clean. I haven't decided yet. Sunday is Mother's Day. I don't think we'll do anything special. I might just continue office stuff and join the weekly game session on my friend C.E.'s Discord server.

We're trying to teach Peanut to go to bed on her own. First night was a struggle. She does okay for naps. She cries for maybe 15 minutes and then curls up with her stuffed animals and drifts off. Hubby laid her down while I was still at work. He heard her coughing and went in to check on her to see a huge mess in her bed and on the floor. She had worked herself up so much that she made herself sick. So, when I came home, he was washing her bedding and was cleaning the floor. Like I said, she's okay for naps but, for some reason, bedtime is different. I wonder if she doesn't like the darker room? All I know is this is going to be a battle of the wills.

But, this is a lesson we should have started sooner. Oh well. We're dealing with it now.

I spent the first 3 weeks of April trying to outline book 5. All the while, I was fighting shiny ideas for future books that want to happen. Which is why I write everything down. Then, I decided to give myself permission to say screw the outline and just draft. And that made a huge difference. I came up with a really spooky idea that I am going to enjoy writing. It's dark, especially for me. But, what can I say? I hang out with a lot of dark fantasy and horror writers.

Wednesday, after my in-laws left, I joined C.E.'s livestream on their YouTube channel. C.E. brought up some kind of disease that involved burrowing worms and I'll spare you more details than that. Most of us were horrified. One girl even took off her headphones so she didn't have to hear. Meanwhile, L, who is a horror writer, leaned in all intrigued. "Oooh, tell me more. This is book plot fuel!" We were all laughing.

Next weekend, we're getting together at my parents house to continue Peanut's birthday celebrations with my sister, brother-in-law, and their kiddos. It'll be only the 4th time they've all seen each other in a year. They're 1, 2, and 3. I have a feeling my mom's dog won't know what to do with 3 high energy toddlers. I hope the weather is nice so they can run around outside.

During the week should be easier. I no longer have to go to work to get tested since I have the vaccine. Thank you Mr. Governor. That saves me a twice weekly 2 hour round trip. I won't burn through gas as quickly and can actually make plans once in a while.

Alright, I have an early morning and a long weekend ahead.

Wednesday, May 12, 2021

So, I have had a mental block due to exhaustion battling a toddler at bed and naptime so I have not been drafting book 5 like I want to. I think I've written a paragraph since Sunday.

BUT, that does not mean I haven't been productive in other ways. Every night, before bed so far this week, I have been making notes in the printouts of the other 4 stories so I am better prepared when full editing time comes. I like to have 30 minutes of no tech time to help me sleep so I'll either read or work on these notes. I highlight places in the double parentheses that need to be fleshed out- which is most of the parts involving magic. As this is fantasy, that's a LOT of purple on the page right now. If I have a placeholder, that's another color. I have the dates, for my reference only, so I marked that so I know to delete in the file sent to critique readers.

I have a list of people I already I want to be my alpha readers. Just want to expand on certain parts and it will still be really rough. But, I trust these people with their feedback. Some I'm thinking of asking have been my closest friends since high school. Some I have met in the past year through AuthorTube from all over the country, and some in Canada.

I've also learned to be too strict with my deadlines. At least for now. Sure, I'm working on this journal regularly and I have a Patreon that I post something on at least every week. But, people are paying for those things. There's a creator/consumer expectation there. My series isn't out yet. Won't be out until 2024. So, as long as I'm doing SOMETHING to move things along, I considered that good progress. I have 4 stories at least in the first draft. Plenty of material to work on when I can't focus on the work in progress. And, sometimes going back to refresh my memory is what my brain needs to keep going. Maybe I'll find a plot thread left dangling or I will have to weave through a change that sparks other ideas.

And, sometimes, the light bulb clicks when I'm not working and I scramble to write the idea down. That's what happened with the series antagonist arc. I was feeding Peanut and all of a sudden, "I need a pen! I need paper!" I scribbled down all I could while my poor 6 month old looked at me like "Mom! We're not done with my sweet potatoes!" But, those moments are rare blessings from the muses as any author will tell you.

I have a section in my Overall notebook called "Prompts and Questions." Something I got the idea for after listening to my friend SW's podcast. Writing down questions like "What if Character X was working with or for the villain?" or "what if Character O had a dark past she didn't want her family to know about?" I also have a ton of prompts on a board on Pinterest and I write down any that catch my fancy at the time. And those prompts can expand into "What Ifs" to fit the story I'm planning.

So, if you're trying to find ideas, maybe give that a try. No harm in it. Just beware the Pinterest Rabbit Hole. It can be very hard to climb out. I do that more than I care to admit.

Tomorrow, Peanut has occupational therapy and then naptime. I think I'll stretch out with my feet up and work on edits while she sleeps. I work this weekend and we have Peanut's party with my parents and sister. Fingers crossed on the weather so the Littles can run around outside together. I've been looking forward to this for weeks.

Sunday, May 16, 2021

So, a lesson I am always being reminded of is the importance of self care. I have lost count of the number of times I've burned myself out to the point of getting sick. I was in youth theater and always had a cold on or near performances. I remember stuffing tissues into the sleeves of my costumes and then spending time backstage blowing my nose so I could be on stage without sniffles. After I had Peanut, I spent that birthday on the couch with a severe migraine. And, one day, I nearly passed out in the NICU from stress and dehydration. I also have anxiety which tells my brain to completely freak out when something goes awry.

These are times when I need to implement the "Fuck It Day." Find an activity that is low stress and do that, to-do list be damned. I'll put on a fun movie for me and Peanut, and Hubby when he's home. Usually anything starring the Minions because Peanut is obsessed. Or Hubby will have Daddy-Daughter time and I'll shut myself away in the office and play a game on my computer. There are also times when I need to get out of the house. I'll get in the car, turn on music or a podcast, and drive.

I had to do some of that on Thursday. I knew Peanut wouldn't nap in her crib. So, I strapped her in the car seat and drove around so she could sleep even for an hour. That usually helps but I nearly wrecked 3 times because of people not paying attention. So, I had a game night.

I did get some writing in the morning for an hour so the day wasn't a complete waste productivity-wise. Small victories, I guess. But, the rest of the day, I needed to take for myself.

As my friend, C.E. says, "Self-care is productivity." There is nothing wrong with it. It is essential function. Especially now. Life is stressful. Global pandemic. Political unrest. Racial violence. The world is nuts. So, taking time to decompress is necessary. For me, that is escaping into fiction. A book, movie, video game, it doesn't matter. Some people walk outside or exercise. Some journal or create art. Some bake. Some are more extroverted and need to be around people. Ways to cope with stress are numerous.

And then today rolled around. Woke up, got some work together, and went to my other job. I've mentioned that I work as a nursing home receptionist on some weekends. As I was going about my opening duties, cleaning, making sure we have a stockpile of masks at the door, members of the health department walked in. They rarely come on weekends and everyone went on alert. I have always wondered if I'm somewhat empathic because I am sensitive to high stress/anxiety situations and I so my own anxiety started to crank up.

However, unlike Thursday, I couldn't take a "Fuck It Day." So, I had to resort to other ways to keep calm. I couldn't work on my book stuff or watch YouTube. But, I could put on a podcast on my phone. I highly recommend "Write Now with Sarah Werner." Breaking my not using real names rule here because I love this podcast and Sarah is a long time friend of mine. She is also one of the sweetest people I have ever had the pleasure to know. Her voice is calming and her episode topics are inspirational and motivational and just a joy to listen to. So, of course, I had her playing in the background in between phone calls and talking to visitors. It helped to pass the time and I could do other productive "life admin." I had to come up with things to talk about with Peanut's pediatrician this week. I went through my planner to figure out my tasks and appointments. I made a list of things to pack for our zoo trip tomorrow. Being productive eases my anxiety a bit, too. I can't just sit in a quiet room staring off into space. I need to keep busy. I need to do something.

And, once I was off work, we had a great afternoon. Went to my parents to celebrate Peanut's birthday with my sister and her family. It's only the 3rd or 4th time the kiddos have all been together. The weather was perfect so we let the kids run around outside. I took so many pictures and we talked and laughed and had cake. It was wonderful.

Tomorrow, we're going to the zoo with my mom and sister. Cleveland zoo is free to county residents on Mondays. It's still a good time of year when the crowds aren't crazy. And, it's such a beautiful area in the springtime as everything turns green and blooms. It will only be for a couple hours. Sis likes to make sure her Littles get their nap times. Although, all 3 of our kids will likely pass out before we're out of the parking lot. And, with my health issues, I know I'll be in pain for days if I push myself to walk all day long. Still building up my mobility.

I shifted gears a little bit with my work and I think I need to sit down and re-evaluate my goals for June and beyond. I went back to book 1 to highlight and make notes to edit the manuscript. Sometimes that helps me connect the dots, fix my continuity, and then I can move on. I have a partial draft of book 5 that I'm trying to work on but for some reason I'm stuck. It's book 3 all over again and I'm trying not to let it stall me. So, we'll see what happens next.

Monday, May 31, 2021

Well, the weekend... happened. It did not go as planned at all. It started Friday. I started having pain in my leg when I got off work. As the weekend went on, it got worse. It was extremely painful. I couldn't even touch it. It was also red and warm. All of that started to scare me. In 2014, I had a severe blood clot in my right leg. And it looked the same.

So, Sunday, I texted Hubby that I was worried so he called his parents to come watch Peanut. When I came home, we went to the Emergency Room. They performed an ultrasound and waited... and waited... and waited.

Then a nurse came in with my discharge papers. No conversation with a doctor about a diagnosis. They said I had a prescription for anti-inflammatory pain medicine at the pharmacy. When I pushed, he just said I had inflammation and swelling in my leg.

Looking back, I should have pushed but I was tired, in pain, and just wanted to go home. They didn't mention a blood clot so that was some relief and I already had an appointment to begin compression therapy so I would just talk to the occupational therapist and my primary care doctor to know exactly what was going on.

I had to work today and managed to get a bit more editing done but not as much as I would have liked. So, I will have to look over my goals for June and beyond.

I need to get book 5 done this month but I am still figuring it out. I did reach out to a writing friend and asked if I could pick her brain one day. The thing that is stalling me is the villain. And, I want this to be really dark and impactful And, L is a brilliant horror writer. She is always sharing her flash fiction and her way with words is just *chef's kiss.* Perfection. So, I know she can help me come up with ideas to pack the necessary punch.

I have a file in one of my organization apps. It has all of my goals and approximate deadlines for the next ten years. Now, things will change, of course, and I don't have everything filled in that far. But, I like having the ability for a long term outlook. I can see how my life changes and adjust as necessary. As of now, I want to publish book 1 of my series in 2024. That will be a year of big milestones. October 2023 will be my 10th anniversary on YouTube. In April 2024, ten years since I started the series. In May, I'll turn 40 years old. (Yikes) And, Peanut will be in kindergarten.

During this time, I will work on edits and I will continue writing the series as much as I can. I also need to pay down my credit card so I can devote it to business expenses.

I'm also learning more and more about the business side of being an author. I have several books on my wish list on this topic. It's a pretty extensive list. I just bought "The Author Business Plan" and the accompanying workbook by Joanna Penn. I haven't had a chance to read them yet. It's a little hard when I'm so exhausted at the end of the day, chasing after Peanut. But I will eventually get to it.

As May comes to a close, I look forward to seeing what the coming months have in store. Summertime, warm weather, and hopefully a lot of adventures with Peanut and Hubby along with being productive on this massive project.

Monday, June 28, 2021

This month has been batty. I worked almost every weekend except the first one and every Friday. Doctor and therapy appointments galore for myself and Peanut. Trying to write and being blocked when it came to book 5. So, I did not get that draft done. I will have to shift things around to complete it in July. I did make some progress this month. I marked up my drafts of books 1 and 2 and nearly finished applying those changes at least to my file of book 1. In July, I'll finish book 1, apply mark ups to book 2, and book 5's draft. Oh, and on top of that, I'm doing World Building Summer Camp through World Anvil.

Yeah, I know it's ambitious to plan all of these things but I think I can do it. Work isn't as crazy this month. I've planned a few writing sprint livestreams on my YouTube channel and I'm always watching or joining on screen of the livestreams my other friends host on their channels. The sprinting method helps with staying focused. Think the Pomodoro Method. Set a timer for 15 or 20 minutes or so, work as much as you can, and then set a shorter timer to take a break. It's amazing what you can get done in a short burst like that.

I'm excited to try World Building Camp. I heard about it through my friend, C.E, one of my writing friends. Every few days throughout July, prompts are announced and then you write an article about your world based on that prompt. It might be a challenge depending on the prompt as my setting is the real world, being in the urban/contemporary fantasy genre. But, it'll force me to get creative. And, C.E. says it doesn't even have to relate to a plot point. So I can really have some fun.

As for getting unstuck, I am going to chat with L and C.E. to see if they can help me untangle some thoughts. Both are great when it comes to the dark and "spoopy" so I am confident they'll be able to help me.

And, then, the end of the month will be amazing. I'm going up to Geneva with Bestie and her daughter for the Great Lakes Medieval Faire. It's our first time going and I have a costume! There is this site that sells fantasy style clothes and it's all gorgeous! I ordered a dress in this beautiful jewel tone green. It was a little snug under the bodice so I ordered some shapewear to "tuck in the things." And, it fits so much better. I also cut back my soda pop intake for most of June and it resulted in losing 3 pounds. In a month, that's not too bad for me.

Since Bestie lives an hour away, she will come stay with us that weekend and we'll drive to the faire. I think it will be a lot of fun. And, I should have my new compression socks pretty broken in so they won't be too uncomfortable.

Geneva is so beautiful, too. Homey small town feel, partly inspiring my own book setting. Geneva-on-the-Lake is my go-to summer spot. The state park has a beautiful beach and there are parks and little tourist spots. I don't get out there enough because it is a bit of a drive but one day I will take Peanut to the beach. And we'll walk around and have some fun.

I'm hoping I can refill my creative well as my writing friends like to say. Being limited in travel abilities the last two years, I'm antsy as hell.

I plan on bringing a notebook in case inspiration strikes. And, definitely bringing my camera to vlog about it.

Friday, July 9, 2021 3PM

Peanut isn't napping but she is in her crib and quiet so I can get some work done. It feels strange having the day off since I worked the past 5 or 6 Fridays in a row. I'll even get to join C.E's writing stream tonight. Hubby said he will be okay with Peanut. She's had plenty of no nap days. Usually he tries to have a chill night with her when she's over tired.

My goal for tonight is to keep writing book 5. I have a few chapters outlined and decided to try to start getting the draft down in my writing program and then handwrite the outline as part of my tech free time before I go to sleep.

Also, I did a thing! On a writing stream last night led by my friend K, I finished applying the changes for book 1 and I sent a link to some of my writing friends. I have not shared my work in so long. I'm kinda nervous. Now, I know these people. One of them is Bestie who has read older versions of this story. But, I have anxiety and so my brain likes to create disasters even when I know better. Although, an artist is very often their own harshest critic.

6PM

This is a first having a 2 part entry but I have a lot to say today. I managed to get some more work done. Peanut finally nodded off a little after 4. (We laid her down at 2) She slept for a little over an hour. Hubby brought home food so we all ate dinner and I jumped online for C.E's Friday night livestream while hubby gave Peanut a bath.

I don't know how much writing I'll do. I may do some admin type things tonight and throughout the weekend. I've been re-evaluating my goals and deadlines and trying to restructure a few things so I can take advantage of Kindle Vella when it comes to my fiction. I'm hoping book 1 will be ready some time next year. I'll release a chapter at a time, how often is to be determined. And, then I can jump into book 2 revisions and so on. If I can time it right, I'll have enough of a time to keep going with writing the series. I'll release it in serialized form and then compile each book so it can be in physical copies.

I don't know how many books there will be. I have ideas for up to 6 so far, I think. Book 5 I am just starting to pin down and book 6 is shaky at best. But, I want it to be a long series. I love this world. I love these characters. Even the awful ones, I love to hate them.

My main character, Tara, has been in my head for 20 years. I created her in high school as an online role play character. Friends and I would do group chats on AOL Instant Messenger and Yahoo Groups forums (oof, I am showing my age there) and write stories together. We went on some crazy adventures including some alternate, evil Sesame Street where Cookie Monster tried to eat Tara because he smelled the cookies in her backpack. And she was scared of Cookie

Monster in our stories for the longest time after. It was funny at the time.

And then there was the fandom hopping storyline. There was a spell that transported the characters into the bodies of characters of different movies and TV shows. Jay and Silent Bob, Power Rangers, and Harry Potter are the ones I remember. This storyline lasted for several weeks in the forums. There was a reason we called the friend who led this story the Spoof Master.

So, when it came time to write this story, I couldn't get Tara out of my head. Some writers don't like to think your characters don't talk to you. They do and she would not shut up. So, she had to be my leading lady in this series. And then everyone else came (mostly) pretty naturally and easily.

The past 8 years have been fun working with this series and I can't wait to see it in print.

On that note, I better get back to work.

Tuesday, July 13, 2021

Kindle Vella launched today! So, some of you are probably reading through that platform. So, HI! And thank you! Or, you could get the full volume... some day. Hopefully not too far in the future. So, to those reading in the future that way, HI and also thank you!

So, I spent the day spamming links all over social media and finding friends that I can support their work. They gave 200 tokens and I'm already making use of mine with multiple stories for author friends.

I am getting down to crunch time with completing this draft for book 5. I got so caught up trying to get book 1 closer to release, I haven't been in a brain space for writing. Except for this chronicle. I did manage to stay off the computer games, although it was tempting. Not going to lie. I'll play Thursday, though. I've been streaming my game play.

I recorded some video this morning for my monthly vlog. I took my makeup down to the basement bathroom and took back my vanity space. I washed all my brushes, threw away some stuff, and reorganized.

I don't wear much makeup anymore. There is just no point for work doing a full face since we still require masks. But, I do like some eye makeup on occasion. Lord knows I have a lot of it. I'm playing with combos for the medieval faire. Only 2 weeks away. Ahh! I have this beautiful eye shadow palatte and I might go get something similar this weekend because I love this line and my sister suggested neutral colors with a pop of sparkle. So, since I have the time, I'm going to try some combinations on days I work or when I do videos. It'll help me figure out what I like and I'm using up my stuff. At least, for videos, I can do a full face of makeup for my videos.

I think I will include some makeup as part of my monthly rewards system. I want a reason to occasionally replenish my stash. So, I am not doing a massive talk like I did in 2019. Threw out stuff from before I got married and I spent over $150 on new stuff... only for the Rona to happen a few months later.

I also got my compression socks. I have to fight for 20 minutes to get them on every day but if it keeps me from having pain and swelling, it's so worth it! I was even able to get flats on the other day! Real shoes! Not sandals! Hubby is going to order a slightly larger pair. One leg has more problems than the other so it's more of a fight and, if I have a crease in the sock, it digs really bad. I don't want any issue if I am at work or walking somewhere. And, I can rotate the socks so they will last longer.

At least my dress will be long enough to mostly cover the socks for the faire. Not that I care what people think.

Tomorrow I really have to work on that draft and get more of those prompts done for summer camp. I should also record some videos. One about this vella project and one with the chronic illness tag my friend M made. I've been promising that I would do it for several weeks now so I will try to do all my recording first thing in the morning. If not tomorrow, then definitely Thursdays.

It's time for bed.

Good night, everyone!

Wednesday, July 14, 2021

I got writing done today! For the first time in weeks, I've touched book 5. I have 6 chapters outlined but I'd like to have a first draft done this month so I am also writing. If I can stay ahead in the outline, I might be able to pull it off. This one is also a multiple point-of-view which is different. I'm getting Tara's sister more into the story... by giving her a whole bunch to deal with that might leave her traumatized. And she's 14 so... stay tuned for that!

Now, it's been a while since I was 14 years old. But, her first chapter was surprisingly fast as I was writing it so maybe it won't be as hard as I originally thought. It took a lot of influence from when I was in 8th grade and modernized it a bit more. So, me at 14 if I had a smart phone? Sort of. Christine is much more extroverted than I am.

I guess the Vella launch yesterday gave me the boost and motivation I needed to get the words down. I want to get as far into this series as I can before I launch the first one then I can edit, release, repeat for a while. I don't know how many books yet. They've been ending up in the 30-40K range, which is more a novella length as opposed to a full novel. But, I don't want to add words that don't fit the story just to hit an arbitrary count. I don't see a problem with a series of 10+ books if they're slightly shorter. As I get my editing and release rhythm down, I can work in writing and continue on as long as I have ideas.

And, boy do I have ideas! I keep having to file away prequel spin-off stories that pop in my head. Either for Gran or my antagonists. Probably leaning more towards Gran because she is incredible and I love her and I can't wait for everyone to read about her. All of the sass. Best comparison, I think is picture Amelia Pond in her mid 80s living in a small town. Still as fiery as ever and taking no bull.

During my work time today, I finished the prologue, wrote chapter 1, and got through a good chunk of chapter 2. I also added my Vella project to my website and did some little admin things. Tomorrow I'm going to finish setting up my basement vanity before Peanut gets up. Then, I have to take Peanut to her speech therapy. We'll come home, have lunch, and then get her down for a nap. While she's down, I'm playing a game called Stardew Valley on livestream and then I'll go watch my friends K and G for their crafting one. K usually then does a writing one after so I can get more words.

At some point, though, I need to keep outlining so I don't get stuck again.

Friday, I have to work so no writing then. I can usually do bits of admin in between work tasks.

Saturday, I am cleaning the office and doing laundry. Sunday, I might take my dad to Church and then I have a ladies group event. We didn't get to have a Christmas party because of the

Rona so we're doing Christmas in July. I have a really cute red dress I could wear to fit the theme.

It's going to be a busy weekend. My office is top priority though. Made a good dent but I need to get rid of the diaper boxes I stocked up on for storage. I want to get to my bookshelf without nearly breaking my neck. I have to put my "work clothes" in my office closet. Keeps some space in the bedroom closet and I can get ready for work in the morning without bothering Hubby. He works Monday through Friday so I try to make sure he sleeps in a bit. He needs the extra energy for Peanut time all day.

Wednesday, July 21, 2021

Found one of the planners I've been neglecting. I bought a five-year planner last year, not knowing the world would catch fire and we'd have a plague. But, I wanted to use it again for better long term planning with my writing and publishing goals. Especially since I want to move things up by a significant amount of time. I'm thinking wide publication will still be in 2024. But, I do want to get my series up on Vella in spring 2022. At least the first book. I guess the serialized version would be called a sort of "soft launch"? Is that the phrase? I'm sure someone will correct me.

This week has been a "weird brain week" and it's only Wednesday! Had a rough day on Monday. Woke up with a sore neck and then Peanut was just in a mood! Cried and crabbed over every little thing. I put her down for her nap and got some work done but I also was feeling a headache building, too.

All that told me maybe I need a break. So, after dinner, we put on a movie and I spent the evening with Peanut and Hubby for the first time in a long time. Around 9, Peanut went to bed and we finished the movie. I did some admin stuff before bed on my tablet but, other than that, I tried to focus on family time. Hubby did, too, so I said I would take Mondays off and we'd make a point to plan some couple time, too. Our anniversary is coming up next month. Date night!

But then, Tuesday morning, I felt this massive wave of guilt for not working for some reason. While, at the same time, I couldn't concentrate! What? I did finally do some work in the evening. My friend, K, hosted a productivity livestream and we played Stardew Valley in between work sprints. It was a lot of fun.

Today was a bit better. Of course, I joined C.E. for their video and caught the end of another. And, those both ended with enough time to watch some TV with Hubby. 2 nights in a row! Record!

Only interruption in the day was when I had to run to work. They started plague testing for everyone again. Twice a week! So, I went today and have to go back Friday. And, that will already be a busy day. Hubby works til 12. We have someone coming to look at one of the trees in the backyard that has some problems and might have to get cut down. In-laws are coming to get Peanut so we can go to the dealership and get me a new vehicle. My lease is almost up and so I'm going to get something new. I know what I want, though, so it shouldn't take that long. Hubby wants to run to the home improvement store and then we'll get some dinner before picking up Squirt and coming home. I work Saturday and Sunday and Saturday is also a family function so it's going to be a crazy next few days.

On top of that, we're getting the house tidied for when Bestie and her oldest come over. We're going to the Great Lakes

Medieval Faire and it's going to be a blast. I'm cleaning out the memory on my phone and made sure I had batteries on hand for my camera. I want to vlog the experience as much as possible. On top of my regular monthly video. But, I'm SO excited for this trip and have started my obsessive monitoring of the weather and praying to whatever higher power who will listen to please let it be a nice couple days. Not to hot and no rain.

It's late so I'm off to bed!

Thursday, July 22, 2021

So, it's not often I have these back to back entries. (Although, I say that now but it's early days) But, I felt reflective and wanted to share with all you lovely readers.

I was sitting at the therapy center waiting for Peanut to come back from her session and marvelling at how far she's come.

Also, a warning. While I will spare the details, I am going to talk about pregnancy complications and having a child in the NICU. If these topics are difficult for you, I am sorry and you should skip to where you see *****.

Today, 2 years ago, was supposed to be Peanut's due date. However, that turned out to not be the case thanks to a variety of factors. Mostly my health issues and then she had a condition called Intrauterine Growth Restriction which meant she was behind in size, although still developing. Because of this and my health issues, I was seeing my regular OB and a high risk one both weekly. That did not help my blood pressure, let me tell you.

End of April, I was sent to stay in the antepartum ward after my blood pressure was scary high. I was only 28 weeks and, while odds were good, they wanted to try to get me as far along as possible. So, Hubby brought me a bunch of clothes and my computer and books. I even asked for my favorite blanket to have a little bit of home comfort and I prepared to stay for however many weeks it would require.

Well, that didn't go as planned. A week into my stay, I started having horrendous pain. Long story short, tests showed I was going into liver failure and it was too dangerous for me and the baby. Time to call the family and off to the operating room for an emergency c-section.

At 6:14 in the morning on May 5, 2019, my baby girl was born. She was so tiny, not much bigger than a Barbie doll. I didn't get to see her until next day once I was able to move around after surgery. And so began 103 of the most stressful days of my life. Traveling to the hospital daily, taking plenty of notes, which I still have somewhere.

Fast forward, we finally got to bring her home. It took a lot of adjusting and a lot of sleep deprivation but we fell into a routine with therapies and specialist appointments. I went back to work part time and eventually was able to start writing again.

Being her first fall and winter, we stayed pretty sheltered. Even had her baptism at home. And, just when we thought we could emerge into the world... 2020 happened.

Fast forward more. Peanut is 2 years old. Small for her age but healthy. Speech and occupational therapy continue. She's happy, friendly, and curious. Loves dancing and playing pretend. She's come so far and I am so proud of my little Feisty Pants. I can't wait to see what the future holds for her.

Being a parent isn't easy. Sleepless nights. Exhausting days. Tears and messes. But, those rewarding moments make it worth it. When she wants to be tickled in the morning. Milestones like her first steps, first words, and going to bed without a pacifier. The way she imitates the characters when we watch her favorite movies. Every day is something new and exciting.

So, happy almost birthday, my sweet girl. You'll do wonders and the world will be better for it.

Monday, July 26, 2021

You know you are an introvert when being around people for a whole weekend leaves you mentally and physically exhausted. I reveled in my "me time" today. I even slept in and took some time during Peanut's nap to catch up on some TV shows I've been recording.

It all started Friday. I ran to work to get my plague test and then Hubby and I went to the car dealer to get a new lease on a vehicle for me. The young man who helped us was very nice and I was able to quickly make a decision and drive off that day. Granted, "quickly" meant 4 hours waiting for people and filling out paperwork but it's done and I don't have to do it again for 4 years.

Saturday, I had to work and then we had a family gathering. Hubby's cousin got married back in April and they wanted to wait til summer to celebrate with everyone. It was nice to catch up with people we hadn't seen in well over a year but I was beat.

Sunday, I had to work and then I took Peanut to see my parents and show off the car. When we got back, I needed to go hide. I hit my people limit and then some. Only human interaction I could handle was through a computer screen. So, I pulled up a game and joined my friends on Discord for our weekly game night. I played until midnight but we were also talking and laughing. And, with that group, it's very easy to lose track of time.

I did not want to get out of bed today. So, I slept in until about 8:30. I showered and got dressed and decided to tidy up the basement so the vanity area is organized for this weekend.

I did make some progress when Peanut napped. My friend, CE, was doing a livestream so I touched book 5 for the first time in at least a week. And, I got my weekly goals up on my crowdfunding page.

After dinner, I joined G and her brother for their discussion on marketing and promotion for writers. I want to go back and watch it all. I came in at the last hour. And then, the "after party" lasted another 3 hours because we just kept talking.

Tomorrow I need to work on more outlining and take care of laundry.

It's the final days until the medieval faire! I am so excited. I have my outfit all set to go. Fresh batteries for my camera, I have even been deleting things off my phone to make room for pictures.

I was productive in other ways today. I made thumbnails for old YouTube videos, mainly my monthly vlog. I even made a special one for the weekend video and had a very specific color scheme. My favorite color is green and Bestie's is pink. I found a pretty background and a bunch of medieval and pirate clipart, changed the coloring to pink and green. It was a lot of fun to make. I am trying to put a more conscious effort into making thumbnail art for my videos. It's better for branding, aesthetically pleasing, and professional looking. I have a pretty small channel but I do enjoy making videos when I can. I do want to move livestreams over to Twitch eventually and then recorded discussions will be my primary content on YouTube. Twitch was made for livestreams and it's also easier to get monetized at 50 followers, not 1000. They're also not as restrictive. YouTube will flag anything or just have the algorithm bury you. Some of my friends have had big success on Twitch. The author community is growing and it's exciting to see.

We'll see what else I can get done this week. I can't believe July is almost over. What is time? Why is it going so fast? I mean, I know many of us would rather skip 2020 but things can slow down a little but. But, maybe this is a "me" problem.

Saturday, August 7, 2021

Well, we are a week into August. The faire happened and it was an absolute blast. And, it gave me a ton of ideas so I am completely rewriting my outline for book 5. I did a ton of worldbuilding and a ton of work on a whole new outline. So, I do need to (again) reconfigure my goals and deadlines. I still want to get book 1 edited starting at the end of this year. It's finding the balance between getting drafted work out for publication and continuing to write new stuff.

The Medieval Faire was fun and exhausting. I also learned not to care about costume accuracy when it comes to shoes. On day 1, I made the mistake of wearing my flats and spent all day walking on unpaved, rocky paths. My feet and back were throbbing! Sunday, I pulled out my tennis shoes. And, while I had to still take frequent breaks, I wasn't in as much pain as Saturday.

They created a whole world setting for this fair. It's set up like a medieval village with crafters and food vendors. There were areas for performers- musicians, comedy acts, magicians.

Something around every corner. The games area was fun. A jousting arena, which sadly we did not catch, the archery range, and knife and ax throwing. I recorded a lot of it and put together a vlog on my YouTube channel. I do need to work on my process of recording things like this but I haven't done a single event vlog in 3 years since I took a trip to the zoo with my friends.

We all dressed up and basically played pretend for 2 days. I was a witch. Bestie was a sorcerer and her daughter was an elf. We had names and everything. It was a lot of fun and helped enhance the experience of being in another world- which triggered the new ideas for my book plot.

And, I wish I could talk more about this story. But, being book 5, I risk massive spoilers for books that aren't out yet. Even when those books are out, how do I know people reading this have read everything? But, I'll share what I can.

In case I haven't mentioned, I'm writing a contemporary(ish) fantasy series. My main protagonist, Tara, goes to a small town to live with her paternal grandmother before she starts college. She finds out she's a witch and magical shenaniganery ensues. After going to the faire, I kept having ideas of being transported to a real medieval style world but with some changes to make it more fantastical. I was even having dreams about it. That told me that it must be written.

So, Wednesday morning, I opened a new document and started outlining. Then I had to leave for my plague test, completely losing my naptime writing session and then lost more time in the evening because Hubby had a meeting. I was more than a little antsy. I got up around 4:30 the next morning to try and make up for it.

I've outlined up to the point where Tara and company enter the world and get separated. I established a new setup on World Anvil to create this kingdom. And, since I put it all this work, I may do a series spin-off focused in this world one day. I don't think it's worth all the work for one book. It's such a fun setting to work on and a ton of potential for stories.

So, in true Me fashion, I bought notebooks for it! Half Price Books sells these *gorgeous* journals with fantasy themed covers so I picked up a few and am using them for all my world notes to be added to World Anvil later. Once I get some more books drafted for the contemporary fantasy, I can shift my focus to the other world for a bit.

I don't want to get ahead of myself and I know this is insanely ambitious. But, I'm not going to lie when I say I'm giddy at all the potential.

I am going to take some time off in the middle of the month. My wedding anniversary is coming up and I've been pestering Hubby for a date night. Even if it's sending Peanut to Grammie's and having ordering take-out from somewhere. That doesn't mean I'll leave my notepad or tablet in the office. If I get an idea, I have to write it down. But, it won't be my usual nighttime routine of writing in my office. I'm pushing for a double date, which is also long overdue.

We're also talking about part time daycare for Peanut. She can start preschool next year but she has been so sheltered her whole life so far. I'd like her to get used to being around other kids. And, my mother-in-law works at the daycare and with her age group. I think that will help a lot, too. It'll make for a busy week. Daycare, therapy, any other appointments or events. It'll be an adjustment for everyone but it'll be good for her and I have some plans of my own.

More on that, though, when the time comes.

Saturday, August 14, 2021

It has been a long day. I couldn't fall asleep until 1:30 and then I got up at 6:15 so that was fun. I had to run some errands before coming home and shutting myself in the office to try and clean. I failed to make a lot of progress but an attempt was made so I mark it as a win.

I also made some marketing images for Instagram while on a friend's livestream. Another bit of productivity.

We had to make a Target run yesterday and I picked up some 5-subject notebooks for my new organization process. Taking a page from Hubby's book and having designated notebooks for things regarding writing and my business. I have one for my crowd funding, publishing, streaming and video creation, branding, and story ideas. I have ideas for more but I was limited on spending until payday this week and that section was pretty picked over because of back to school shoppers.

I have a list going for a big office supply refresh but I'm waiting for Halloween stuff to be out. Because Halloween decor is not seasonal for this fantasy writer. Give me all the witches, black cats, ghosties. And, if I can find dragons to throw into the mix, even better. I have an inspiration table in the corner of my office with all manner of things. A candle, a wooden Madonna and Child figure, a crystal ball, a ceramic dragon hatchling, and my oracle and Tarot decks that I have no idea how to use.

As I keep working on the declutter, I keep getting ideas on how to improve my space visually and functionally. With the amount of livestreams I host and participate in, I want to position things so it looks good on camera. When I do recorded videos, I use my rolltop desk as my background so I am displaying various items I enjoy and I have a letter board for messages based on video topics.

Functionally, I just want all the things in easy reach for whatever I'm working on. And, I don't want to break my neck in the process. Partly why I want a wireless keyboard- one less cord. I saw this beautiful one that looks like a typewriter. It's in my wish list and might be a reward for myself down the road. Either monthly or a milestone reward like when I publish the first of my series or 10 Years on YouTube. I'll find a reason to justify it.

I am up to chapter 12 in my outline. My momentum is slowing and I don't like it! I do not like it at all. To be fair, we have had a health crisis in the family. (It is not the plague but it's still pretty serious) So, that added some stress and put me in a head space that cued my anxiety. So, I resolved to go easy on things and be happy with whatever gets accomplished.

I did add a lot of files for world building and starting that organization process counts. I keep looking at my deadline list and just... cue the sighs of frustration. I am getting better but I am not quite where I want to be with keeping on task. It is a problem I have had since I was a kid. And that leads to all of the internal guilt.

I am going to break my rule about naming names because she deserves all the love. My friend, Sarah Werner, has a podcast called "Write Now." She has an episode on writer guilt that I occasionally go back to when I need it. I just listened again recently. She talks about guilt being a huge part of our culture, at least in the Great Lakes Region of the US where we grew up. Laying on the guilt when expectations aren't met. And, it starts in childhood for a lot of people, albeit not always intentionally and we internalize it. I need to work on that. One of the many things I want to work on in my life. I don't want to guilt Peanut like some people, teachers in particular, guilted me because it has an impact. I really hate when people say "Why can't you be more like (insert comparisons here)."

Before I get on a soapbox, I need to take my sleep deprived self to bed.

Tuesday, September 7, 2021

So, it's been a hot minute since my last entry. Because the past few weeks have been... a time. I'm not going to say much about it right now. But, because of things happening, my goals got tossed out the window for a while. It's nobody's fault. Things happen. I am just glad I don't have any publisher deadlines or anything like that.

So, summer is almost over. I can't believe it. Another summer gone way too fast. I didn't make it to Bestie's to go to the pool. I didn't get to take Peanut to the beach. And, the Plague rages on so there's not much of anything going on still. School has started, even for Peanut. Well, it's daycare a couple times a week. But, it'll help get her started for school. And, she's only going at first on days when Hubby doesn't work a full day so if I get held up with things he can go get her.

Outline for book 5 is making progress, though. Even if it is crazily slower than I'd like. I think I like the direction I'm considering going. I get to play with a couple characters that haven't had a major role in the series thus far. And, I created a whole new world that may result in its own series if I can come up with enough stories for it. This world is much more fantastical than my primary series, which is contemporary/urban fantasy. I was playing with world building and having a lot of fun. I filled a notebook with ideas and histories and building and layouts. There was one night when I did not get to bed until 1 a.m.

Back on book 1, I have received some feedback from friends. There is one part I need to go in and flesh out because it's just my "This thing happens but I don't know how to write it out" sort of notes. It's the only part of the book that is not completely written.

I'm still thinking about a serialized release in 2022. All depends on funds so I can hire an editor. Fingers crossed it's the end of this year I can at least contact the editor in mind. I'm waiting on the feedback to make a few more changes if needed and just to get some more eyes on it. Since that kinda hasn't happened in a couple years. Definitely before I did the major rewrite.

Once I get feedback and book 1 to the editor, I think I'll be able to move on fixing up the other books I've written so far. I know books 3 and 4 need a LOT of work. Those drafts are not very long in comparison to the first 2 and there are more parts that are just notes than fully written out scenes. I sort of wrote those stories in a hurry, though, just so I could make progress. But, first drafts aren't meant to be perfect. Editing exists for a reason.

Like I said before, goals are kinda up in the air for a while because life things. But, I do want to get the outline for book 5 done this month. Worse case scenario, October. And then, maybe first draft will be my National Novel Writing Month project.

I'm also looking ahead to 2022. So much I wanted to do this year that I didn't get to so I am determined to do all the things next year, come hell or high water. Including a retreat with some of my writing friends. I think we were talking about somewhere near Salem? Or, that's the location some shared in our chat about it. And, I want to take what I am calling a "Mom-cation" with my best friend. I think we both need it. A few days away, even if it is just a long weekend. We wanted to do it last year and... well, we all know what happened.

Anyway, it's late. I'm exhausted.

Monday, September 20, 2021

So, I have been struggling to work on anything in recent weeks. I mentioned in the last entry that I have had a lot going on so it is really hard to focus but I did manage to edit a bit yesterday. I took out my highlighters and started marking up the broad parts in books 2 through 4. Mainly, all of the parts where I need to fill in and flesh out details. My manuscript looks like it is bleeding from all the red highlighters.

I also made copies of book 1 on Google Docs to send to friends. One of my friends suggested that after one of her alpha readers overloaded her document with comments! I am a little nervous and I am trying not to obsessively refresh the page waiting for comments but it is so hard! When your writing was held up in school as the example of what not to do, it has an impact on your self esteem as a writer. Yes, that was twenty years ago and it was a research paper, not fiction, and I've grown a lot in developing my craft since then. Point still stands. I am always anxious. Even when I know better. One of the joys of having chronic anxiety.

The other thing I started doing is what my friend C.E. calls Anxiety Art. I picked up some thin canvases, new paints, and brushes, and started painting again. I made a cute little picture for Halloween. It's a dark night with a house on a hill, a jack-o-lantern, and a ghost. Not done yet. But, it has turned out cute so far. I have some paint along tutorials saved on YouTube as well to help me get some practice. Maybe one day I will add some to my shop on Ko-Fi, the crowdfunding platform I am on. I wonder if I have canvases at my parents house still. I am trying to use what I already have before justifying buying more. I used to paint quite a bit. Usually abstract but I would like to practice other things as well. And with everything going on right now, it is nice to hide away and make something beautiful. I did some painting when Peanut was in NICU. They had an art therapy class and it was a lot of fun. I would look for motivational quotes to use with a decorative background.

There is one thing I want to try and make and I know it is going to take a lot of practice. It is a dream scene from book 1 of my series. It is a bonfire in the middle of a clearing with people dancing around it. It appears in chapter 1 and is the first of many dreams/visions/whatever that my main character has throughout the series and I would just love it on my wall. I don't know if I can do justice to the image in my head but I am going to try. At one point, I wanted that scene to be my book cover but I don't know if it will fit the modern setting. It does appear later in the book and just the clearing, no fire, before the end, so maybe?

Also, I got my 2022 planners today. And, thanks to sales, some new sticker books. And, yes, planners. Plural. I will be using 3 next year. One is a giant catch-all for home stuff. I even found this household expansion that has meal planning and cleaning and a section for budgets. I added a section for party planning and projects. And then two are for work. One is for social media and the other is for goals. It's pretty typical for me and, somehow, I am able to keep up with them all… usually.

It gives the illusion that I am organized anyway. I've always enjoyed planners. And writing things down helps me retain it better. I could never keep up with things on my phone. I think I only use my Google calendar I can share work and appointments with my family. I have plans and ideas for the coming year and I'm really excited.

Thursday, September 30, 2021

Trigger warning for cancer, bereavement, loss, mourning

It is hard to believe I felt hopeful about anything just ten short days ago. Talking about getting feedback and all the plans I wanted to make. It all came to a screeching halt just a couple days later.

I should have picked up that something was going on. Not only did I get up well before my alarm, I had this overwhelming urge to stay busy- so much so that I could not settle on anything. I'd start making notes and then I would play with promo images and I had to have either a YouTube video or music on. No silence.

Suddenly, the doorbell rang. Now, we live in a quiet area. Nobody comes around unless they're selling something so I almost ignored the alert on my phone until I saw who it was. I am surprised I did not wake Peanut the way I stampeded down the hall to unlock the front door. My mom and sister stood there, tears in their eyes holding donuts and coffee and I lost it. They didn't even have to say a word I knew.

My dad was gone.

He had been battling cancer for nearly a year and that day he went home to God. We cried and hugged. I called Hubby and then we had to start telling people and making arrangements. Fortunately, he had a lot of his wishes laid out already. So all we had to do was contact the necessary people to get everything finalized. And to spread the word to family and friends.

The week progressed in a kind of haze. Condolences, tears, meeting with my dad's friends in the clergy to help with services and remembering. We spent a whole day sorting pictures and talking about stories we have of Dad. Like going fishing at our special spot and catching Sis trying to set our bait free. Or all the meals he made for Church functions. "If the food's not good, I won't be there." How he would sing Elvis karaoke and all the ladies at the senior center would swoon at his gorgeous baritone voice. He even sang the song Hubby and I danced to for the first time as husband and wife.

And, he did so much in his life to have all those stories. Police officer, paramedic, Army vet, business man, truck driver, Deacon, senior center coordinator, volunteer chef. All of that on top of being a son, husband, father, including pet daddy, brother, uncle, and Papa (grandpa) to his 3 favorite people.

And, he was never one to back down from a challenge. Whether that's standing in a thunderstorm trying to pour concrete or his own cancer diagnosis. When they told him the odds were against him, he said, "So what are we gonna do about it? If you think I'm going to just roll over and let it take me, get out of here and find me someone who'll have a treatment plan." Basically, "I came into this world kicking and screaming and that's how I plan to leave it."

And, while it was not kicking and screaming, he did fight as hard as he could until he couldn't anymore. And, my mom was with him. He was not alone so I can find some solace in that.

So, Wednesday came and went in a puffy-eyed blur. The evening prayer service was beautiful. My sister surprised everyone by giving the eulogy. So many people came to pay their respects. People he knew from before I was born that we had never met. It was heartwarming and also an introvert's nightmare. I can fake being an extrovert. I get that from both my parents. Especially around people we connect with. But, it's draining. And, at something so emotionally heightened as this, even more so. I was thankful my in-laws offered to take Peanut for the night.

Today was Mass and cemetery stuff and we laid him to rest near his parents and one of his brothers. More visiting with family and then Hubby and I went to get Peanut. Hubby was fighting seasonal sinus stuff so I took Peanut to see my mom for a couple hours.

Now I am back home, in bed. Hubby is sawing logs next to me and Peanut is fast asleep in her room in whatever happy little dreamland she goes to. And, I am trying to comprehend this new normal we are now faced with. Holding back every time I want to reach for my phone to ask him a question. Dealing with the anger, sadness, confusion, just overall lacking of a reason why fueling the feels in my brain. All the "What if" and "Coulda been." The "Why hadn't I said/done XYZ when I had the chance?"

I guess it's one of those great mysteries we have to deal with in our own time. I will say, I didn't expect to write about it here but, as I bring this entry to a close, it's helped start the process of healing. Writing is my outlet. My dad was one of my biggest cheerleaders when it came to my writing. So, I really want to make him proud when I get to the point of releasing my fiction.

I really need to get some sleep now. I have another long weekend ahead.

Wednesday, October 6, 2021

Today was an alright day. I got Peanut off to daycare, put laundry away that has been in baskets for nearly a month, even did my seasonal swap. It was sad putting away summer things, though. Once again, an under-eventful summer has come and gone. The world continues to be ravaged by Plague so that doesn't help. But, it also was a very rainy summer.

I did have to run to work for a meeting. Then, I picked up a cake and we had a little party for Hubby's birthday today. He has a milestone next year so I should start tossing around party ideas and reach out to his parents and brother to help plot and plan.

It felt good to be working again. I'm reading through book 1 again and making notes. Missed spelling here, wrong word used here, clarify something there. I have made almost 90 notations in the 12 chapters I've read out of a total of 18. Also, other people are reading it! Yikes! Three friends have copies to leave comments on and I am so nervous. Not many people have read it in the 8 years I've been writing and these friends have a really good critical eye. I know I'll get great feedback.

I also reached out to an editor who came highly recommended and has worked with a number of friends. I got a cost quote and we'll figure out a time after the holidays to work together! So... I could maybe plan a release in 2022? Maybe? At least starting in serialized form. I'm hoping for May. I have a sticky note on my birthday as a possible release goal. And, I don't have to work at day job that weekend so all the livestreaming and events! And, when I do a compiled release with a physical copy, it's really going to be a party. Fingers crossed the plague subsides by then. I want to reach out to a bookstore to hold a launch event. And, then there's conventions and events like the arts festival in the town I grew up in. Once the library starts having in person, they hold talks and events for traditional and self published authors. Panels and at least 2 conferences. And I will probably reach out to friends about conventions and we can all meet up, maybe share table costs. I looked into something huge like the Wizard World Comic Cons and it was close to $1000 to have a table for the weekend. Not counting hotel, gas for travel, copies of books, promo and swag.

So, now I have a list of things to do to get this going. Cover, getting in place any legal and business stuff. I have plenty of people who can help with that.

My latest non-writing challenge has been toddler tantrums. Oh. My. Word! I don't know if it's a badly timed phase or all of the recent changes in the past month. But, simple, every day things like sitting at the table for dinner or finishing a puzzle have become meltdown worthy. Screaming, biting, throwing, the whole nine yards. It has to be part of where the Terrible Twos came from. I have talked with her speech therapist because the tantrums during sessions are hindering her progress. (I've mentioned she was a preemie, I think, so she's speech delayed) I feel like we're going through sleep training again, listening to her cry from down the hall until she falls asleep.

I talked about it with a friend and we agree part of it is stress. Hubby and I have been stressed with my being with my Dad while he was in his final weeks so Hubby had to help extra around the house. She can't communicate that she's upset so it's frayed nerves all around. May be, according to this friend, why she thrives at daycare. It's her escape from the stress at home. We don't mean for it to be stressful but things happen and we have to figure out ways to deal.

I'm hoping we will find whatever the new normal is and the stress lowers. It will take time as Hubby and I are constantly reminding each other.

I think I am going to take work on the road at some point over the weekend. I have a little cash stored away so I might take my read through, go find a coffee shop, and get a couple hours of work in at a different environment for the first time in... well, 2 years. My ear buds are broken so that means I couldn't listen to music but it's not a requirement to focus. I can make my reading notes or work on organizing other things.

Sadly, Bestie will be at Scout camp with her boys. I'd love to go visit her for a day. And, I need her husband's help on my website. It's... well, it's bland. But, I haven't quite mastered changing the colors. I will have to add that to my list as well. So much to do if I'm considering this launch for when I want it. Maybe that will be my other focus this weekend. Sort out to-dos, clean my office because it looks like it exploded, website, and coordinate with Sis to do updated photos.

I can't think of any of that now or I won't sleep. So I am off to unwind for a bit then back at it in the morning.

Saturday, October 9, 2021

I hope this becomes a common thing having updates more frequently. I am kinda living for it right now. I finished my read through notes for book 1 of my fantasy series last night. Got up today and thought, "I'm off this weekend. I am going to take Saturday and Sunday to apply these changes and send copies for my 3 friends who are beta reading." Well… I did it all today. 18 chapters! Just under 35,000 words in the whole manuscript with a couple gaps to fill in after feedback but I started at 7:30 this morning and ended around 4:00. And, I remembered to take a lunch break, which I don't often do when I get into this sort of work flow. Then, I ran to the library and managed to print the draft with 2 minutes to spare before everything shut off for the day.

I should have probably taken more breaks and had more water. I feel some cramping in my leg. Charlie Horse at 4 a.m. anyone? But, I felt so energized! I didn't want to stop. I know I'll sleep good tonight. And I'll be back at it in the morning. Depending on when I get up, I can do some work before I get

Peanut out of bed, spend some time with her and Hubby, and then do my planned work.

I also managed to do some admin before I ended for the night. I finally updated my website and added some things to my crowdfunding page.

Tomorrow I really need to knock out cleaning and organizing. I have books and papers scattered about. I should finally set up my printer, even if I don't have any paper and ink yet. And, I have a bunch of things I can store in the basement.

While waiting for feedback from my friends, I am going to start looking over book 2. I have my highlighter color key ready. It seemed to work for book 1. Highlight and notation numbers on the printout and then detailed notes corresponding to those in a big notebook. It is a good thing I have a ton of highlighters because, after book 2, the amount of work needed increases dramatically. I could very well run out of ink. I have more gaps to fill in for books 3 and 4. But, I am giving myself to the end of the year to do all this work and then get back to drafting as much as possible in 2022. I am giving myself 2 months per book to have at least a first draft so I should have up to book 10 planned by the end of the year.

If all goes as planned, by May, book 1 should be up on Vella and possible book 2 at some point later in the year. Full release I'm thinking 2023. Now, this is just what I would like to have happen. I have had things blow up in my face so I am always hesitant to make hard deadlines unless I know I can pull it off. With Peanut now being in daycare a couple days a week, that gives me more work time and, other than when I am a guest on someone's livestream video, I can take an evening or *gasp* a whole day off for family time. Or, *double gasp* time for myself as self care!

I am breaking my rule of no real names but I love the Write Now Podcast by my friend, Sarah Werner. One of her more recent episodes is all about taking down hustle culture. The whole concept of constant hustle and you MUST always be productive every day to have any worth. On top of that, when something gets in your way to keep you from working, you must double or triple down to "catch up" on what you didn't do. And, that's just toxic and self destructive. It's how you lead to severe burnout. And that can be detrimental to your health.

I have had burnout at various points throughout my life. When I was in youth theater, there was one production where I was student director. Juggling that and being in 7th grade, I had a lot going on and, come performance time, I got really sick. I actually had tissue shoved up the sleeves of my costume and, every time I was off stage, I was blowing my nose. When Peanut was in NICU, I nearly passed out in the unit because I was exhausted and dehydrated. Fortunately, I have learned my symptoms. Usually I start to get a headache and an upset stomach. When that happens, I'll have a gaming day or I'll take Peanut to a park. Sometimes, I'll go for a drive and have some Introvert Time. Or, if it's really bad, I'll take a nap. And all of this has helped me learn to keep my goals flexible. I have nobody to answer to but me. So, if I'm sick, I can't work. I've tried. It doesn't end well.

Sarah has a few episodes along the same line dealing with hustle and burnout. She is also just a lovely, wholesome human.

I need to review my goals for tomorrow and the coming week and then, maybe, I'll be able to rest.

Friday, October 15, 2021

Hello again, friends,

Well, I started on Wednesday reading through book 2 while I wait for feedback on the first one. I had a Facebook post pop up in my memories about the first time I outlined this story in 2014. I was ready to bust out an outline for book 3 and then write both for National Novel Writing Month in November. Oh, how naive I was. Book 3 turned out to be a years long struggle to nail down. I didn't get something I sorta liked until this year, after a major rewrite of books one and two! Then, book 4 came surprisingly easy and all attempts to outline and draft book 5... let's just say life has some really bad timing. Part of the reason I'm taking a break from drafting and focusing on edits through the end of this year.

But that should make things better and, maybe easier? At least everything will be fresh in my head and I'll have better notes. I also have been working on a map of my little town that I made up. I don't know if that is something I'll share or if I'll keep it for my own reference. Maybe one day I'll decide. I have to finish it first. I also might see if Hubby will help me make some models. I'd like to do a model of Gran's house and possibly a layout of the college but we'll see how he suggests we do it so I can decorate it. I'm tempted to get a bunch of table top gaming pieces but those are mostly fantasy themed so I don't know how that will work out. And, it'll cost a pretty penny.

I managed to knock out 6 chapters this week. But, I had quite a bit going on. I was on a panel discussion on Monday on YouTube. We talked about fantasy and sci-fi with a bunch of other writers and it was wonderful. Tuesday was my night off and Wednesday I couldn't focus until evening. Partly since I was browsing an IT site for keyboards and other tech for my office. I found 2 keyboards that I really like. We'll see how fast I can save up for them. I was finally able to knock out more Wednesday night and Thursday. Hoping to finish making notes for the remaining 4 chapters over the weekend. And, unlike with book 1, I am going to slowly apply the changes.

Doing book 1 all in one day was a mistake and I felt it for most of the week. Also, there are many more gaps that need to be filled in and expanded upon. The current draft is just under 20,000 words and I'd like to add at least another few thousand to beef it up a bit more. The last chapter especially is mostly ((concept here)) and is only about 200 words. Needs some major work.

I am getting back into having my music on when I work. I can't have noise canceling headphones so I can keep an ear out for if Peanut is in her crib and needs me. Although, Hubby still is able to sneak up on me if I have it loud enough because he is frustratingly sneaky and has scared me while on a video stream before. But, the music does help me get into the mood of a story.

I have a massive playlist with almost 2600 songs that are all fantastical or spooky themed that I listen to during my morning prep work or if I'm doing something not specifically story related. If the right song comes on, I'll add it to a book specific playlist. Some songs are repeated on all of the ones I have set up because they have a nice tone or beat for just about anything while the rest fit more specific details, like the time of year the story takes place. So, book 1 is in the summer time. So, the music is mostly light and fun and have titles referring to beach trips and picnics. Book 3 is Halloween so it's all of the spooky and fall themed. Book 4 is Christmas time so winter. And then I'll add music for spell work scenes and battling the big bad of the story. You get the idea. They're all private for right now except for the huge one but, maybe, as the books come out, I'll make them public.

It has been fun and relaxing putting those playlists together. Like I said, they help me focus. That's always a problem for me but I'm getting better. I try to only have certain apps and sites open when I work. No social media except Twitch or YouTube. But, that's because, if I'm not streaming myself, I'm usually watching someone's livestream and doing the work sprints.

The other task I need to work on this weekend is a series of graphics for an Instagram challenge for National Novel Writing Month. I'm not officially participating this year since editing is my focus but the challenge sounded fun so I decided to give it a go to boost my presence on Insta.

It's going to be a busy weekend with the tasks planned and some family stuff. We have a football party at my sister's house. And, my mom found Peanut a new shirt for our NFL team! So, I'll be meeting Hubby at my sister's house after work on Sunday. She lives, maybe, 10 minutes from where I work. There's no point in going from work, 40 minutes back home, grabbing Hubby and Peanut, and driving back. So, I said I would help with party prep and they'd meet me after Peanut is up from her nap. My aunt is also going to trim Peanut's hair so she looks nice for picture day on Tuesday! I didn't know daycare centers did picture day. But, I suppose it's good practice for school.

Alright. Time to do some edits! We'll see how much I can get done and still make it to bed at a reasonable hour. Seeing as my alarm is set to go off at 5 a.m. Although, I know me. If Hubby doesn't help me drag myself out of bed, I'll hit the snooze until 6:30 and then scramble to get out the door in time. But, someday, I won't have to do that anymore. Ultimate goal is to make double what I make at this job so I can quit and have the financial flexibility to manage my business and help with household expenses.

Sunday, October 17, 2021

I'm back!

And, I have thoughts. So many thoughts. It is early(ish) morning- about 8:30 so early for some. I'm sitting at my weekend job with one of my favorite YouTube channels playing as background noise.

I spent yesterday when I got home cleaning my office. I came across my paints and a few blank canvases. I decided to have some fun once I made a dent in cleaning and also see if those paints were still good before I justified spending money on fresh stuff. It was a mixed bag. Some were still pretty good. Some were really thick or had separated over time from lack of use. I also had a few partially full bottles of the same color so I combined them. Once I did that, I looked up some easy things I could copy from sight and lost myself in it. It took some time as I waited for layers to dry but it was a lot of fun. Now, I'm not an artist. I can barely draw stick people. The drawing and painting is more my sister's strength. But, I am proud of the result. I might add some detail either tonight after the family party or tomorrow. I'm also tempted to go to the store and get some more canvas. And, I could use some brush cleaner.

Anyway, I painted until I had no clean brushes left. I let them soak in some soapy water and went to bed. And, that is when I started having a bunch of crazy dreams. I don't remember much beyond some image flashes here and there but I actually woke up before my alarm with a story idea that I am going to try and thought dump when I'm done writing this. A lot of people talk about refilling their creative well in order to keep being creative themselves. They'll read or watch a movie or TV show to try and spark an idea where they're stuck. And, sometimes you need to create in a different way. Some of my friends make music or draw. Some even write fanfic. Apparently, the spark I needed was from painting. And, I know this could be useful because it's 3 hours later and I still have it rolling around in my brain. As opposed to vanishing before I got in the car.

After I showered and got dressed, I sat in my office for a few minutes to finish waking up. And, I know some people aren't going to buy into what I have to say next but I find these things fascinating so I'm going to talk about it anyway.

I have this Literary Witches Oracle deck. I found it at the medieval faire over the summer and had to snatch it up because I am a writer, I love witchy stuff, and the art style is really cool. There are two types of cards. "The Witches" are writers or poets like Mary Shelley, Agatha Christie, and Maya Angelou. The other cards are "The Items." These are prominent things that pop up in the writings of "the Witches." Like, candles, animals, food, plants. And, each card has a couple key words or phrases associated with them.

Each morning, I've been picking a single card. This is meant to be a reflective exercise according to the guidebook that went along with the deck. How do the words or phrases apply to your day?

Well, I drew the "Ghost." It actually kinda jumped out while I was shuffling. And, some of my friends who are more knowledgeable in Tarot and Oracle say that those are the cards you're supposed to add to your draw. A sort of "The Universe (whatever you may choose to call your dedicated higher power) chose this for you." The words on this particular card are "Memories, What haunts you, and Unfinished Business." And that is when I really started to have more thoughts because these words have a lot of application to my life at present.

Memories was easy. We're entering our first year of holidays without my dad and memories and stories have been a major coping mechanism. Almost every time I've streamed with my friends, something has prompted a memory that I've shared.

"Unfinished business" and "What haunts you" can go hand in hand. I make no secret that I have chronic anxiety so anything can get me worrying because that is how my brain works. I am learning how to cope but the struggle is real. When the overwhelm triggers an overly emotional response, I have to bail which leads to unfinished tasks all over the place. Laundry half put away, the continuous challenge of cleaning my office, and 4, soon to be 5, books I've been working on for nearly a decade. Because the thought of publishing, while exciting and something I have been dreaming of for years, is freaking terrifying! Like, I actually wrote in my publishing task list "Panic, release, panic more, pass out." I'm already anticipating the anxiety.

This series is a long time labor of love and I want readers to enjoy it as well. I also know that it will be on the Internet and that trolls abound. I'm half expecting someone giving me a 1 star review for the sake of nitpicking something completely unrelated to the story. I think I can handle that. Also, some criticism becomes a humorous badge of honor. One lady in a mom writer group I'm in wrote a Good Omens style story and a local church bought 200 copies to burn. And, she reveled in it. Because it's ridiculous that these people got so butt-hurt over a piece of fiction and she still got paid.

I still have some other things to think about but I really want to get into planning this story with the dream ideas before I jump back into edits so I'll leave it here.

Friday, October 29, 2021

So... yesterday happened. Wednesday I had a doctor appointment and got my plague booster. I woke up yesterday, my arm was still sore but I felt okay. I took Peanut to Occupational Therapy, cleaned out my car, laid Peanut down for a nap, and was ready to settle in to work. And then the body aches and chills hit me. Slowly at first and then I just felt like crap. I texted Hubby and dragged myself back to bed.

I slept from 4 to about 7. I got up, showered, had some food and tried to work but my brain was not having it. So, I went back to sleep around 9:30 and slept until 5 this morning.

I think it was a combination of the side effects and too many late nights and early mornings combining for all of the burnout. Even Hubby agreed. I was long overdue for a break. And, I felt better after getting some rest. I was a little sluggish this morning but once I got Peanut off to school and ran errands, I was starting to feel better. I managed to apply markups for half of book 2 today!

I work the other job this weekend so it will probably be an admin to-do list. Or, I'll play around with some character brainstorming. Haven't decided yet. And then, Monday, a bunch of writers on Twitch are hosting a relay for the start of National Novel Writing Month. So, I can easily knock out the remaining six chapters by lunch. Then, I have to find time to get to the library so I can print the updated draft.

Applying changes to book 3 is going to take a LOT of work. Most of the mark up notes are "expand details" or "show, don't tell." The plight of a chronic underwriter.

I should be getting feedback from one of my beta readers this weekend for book 1. So, that is terrifying... I mean exciting! Waiting on 2 other friends then I can do another draft and send it off to the editor after the holidays! Also, a terrifying thought but, if it helps me make my book the best it can be then that is what I have to do. I felt a little better after the editor explained their process and that includes a written report and a voice call to go through everything and clarify anything I may not understand in the report.

I am looking forward to Halloween. It's Halloween! We got Peanut a minion costume and she looks so stinking cute. She has gray glasses that go perfect with the outfit. Going over my mom's after naptime. We might try trick-or-treating but it might depend on how many houses have their lights on and the weather. Halloween in Northern Ohio can be unpredictable. I've gone out in a blizzard on numerous occasions. Pro tip: A full face painted green for a witch costume is not a good idea when it snows because ouch!

I am contemplating doing a daily vlog for November. I am not sure I can pull it off or how I want to release it. I could do shorts every day or I could compile them all into a single video at the end of the month. I am not participating in Writing Month but I wanted to share my progress on my edits and keeping up the momentum that happens during Writing Month. Also, it's a good way to cheer on my friends who are actually writing if I take part in the things. Partly why I'm watching the relay on Monday. It's going to be fun. I usually enjoy how everyone comes together in November.

Sunday, October 31, 2021
HALLOWEEN

Happy Spooky Day! I love Halloween. I start listening to Halloween music in early September. It's great. Even better when Peanut dances along. I have it timed out to know that we can listen to the Ghostbusters theme twice on the drive to Daycare.

Today, I got dressed up in this gorgeous green gown with huge bell sleeves. I found a prop staff and a plastic dagger (that I kept home) and put on some sparkly makeup to complete the look for work. When I got home, I rested for a bit and then took Peanut to my mom's for her first trick-or-treat outing! My mom walked with Peanut while I stayed and passed out candy. Peanut had her little Minion costume and loved being outside seeing all the other kids.

She got a ton of candy. Some of it is going into my snack stash because she's so young. So, Hubby and I will share.

While I was at work, I got some character notes done. I'm fleshing out on a D&D character for whenever I'm able to join a campaign with Bestie. She is also going to be my character to play when we go to the Great Lakes Medieval Faire next year. I want to vlog in character next time. Her name is Brigid Roseberg, a socially awkward sorcerer on a lifelong mission of learning and self betterment. At least, that is what I have so far based on the prompts offered with the character app I have. I am going to try and plan something with Bestie next weekend. I am overdue for a visit anyway and the more she talks about her D&D sessions, the more I want to learn. And, who knows. It may spark some story ideas.

I can't believe it's almost the end of 2021. I remember thinking this year had such potential to be amazing. And, I'm not discounting all of the positives. I've been crazy productive. We have been able to see family more since the vaccines came out. Peanut is thriving and hitting milestones left, right, and center. There's still a lot more that I wish had happened and, well, I'd rather forget all of September. I have already started looking ahead at 2022. So many plans, so many ideas.

The biggest one is getting my novel up on Vella once it's edited. I need to come up with a fun cover idea. I might reach out to my friend who is a brilliant cover designer to see if I can commission something from them. This person is also one of my beta readers so maybe they'll have some ideas after reading the book.

Once I am done self editing through book 4, I may be able to keep going with the rest of the series. I have been stuck on book 5 for a while. I don't want to be in a situation like I was with book 3, struggling for years before getting an idea down on paper. Maybe I'll take some time to brainstorm a better direction for the series as a whole and then I can break it down into each book. That might make it easier to at least outline and draft however far I need to go next year.

Since some of my books are comparatively short, I thought a long series would be fun to write. I'm not sure how many but I have enough notebooks set aside to write for a long time. Also, back to school sales are great to stock up on office supplies.

Anyway, I hope you all had a safe and happy Halloween if you celebrate it. If you're doing National Novel Writing Month, please remember to pace yourself. Don't burn out. That would be bad. Drink plenty of water. Eat something other than leftover Halloween candy. And, have fun!

Wednesday, November 10, 2021

I had so many plans for November. I have half of book 2 edited and managed to expand it quite a bit. (It's still way too short but I have six more chapters to work on) But, by the middle of the first week, all productivity screeched to a halt. We all started feeling sniffly, which is to be expected this time of year. Ohio is notorious for having dramatic weather changes in spring and fall, going from near summer weather to ice cold and frost, sometimes even snow, in a single day.

But, then poor Peanut wouldn't sleep and she kept holding her ears. She was coughing up a storm and was just miserable. She already had a regular checkup scheduled so we took her in and found out she had a raging ear infection and they ran a bunch of tests to rule out pneumonia, flu, RSV, and the plague. The doctor gave us medication through a nebulizer to help her cough as well as antibiotics. Spent the weekend sleeping mostly. Well, Hubby and Peanut did a lot of sleeping. I napped here and there. By Monday, Peanut was feeling a lot better. Hubby and I are still battling a bit. Congestion just won't quite go away.

Having a brain full of cold medication, I have not been in a head space to write anything new or to work on edits. So, to still try to be productive, I've been working in my planner for 2022. With another year not going as planned, I am ready to look ahead and try again. I'm playing around with a new layout for my writing work planner and I'm really enjoying it. Another bonus is the color scheme is my favorite colors. Lots of greens and blues and it's really pretty. I have almost the whole year set up, at least with note cards and sticky notes, with the goals I want to accomplish. Not writing anything down on the actual page just yet because life can happen so I want to be ready in case things have to shift. I marked out all of my work weekends for the part time job. I set up my budget and financial goals so I can keep track of royalties. And, had some fun decorating because why not.

I could, once again, be planning way too much. I have this really bad habit of being ridiculously ambitious and then crash and burn. But, I have a few big things I want to accomplish. The first is release books 1 and 2 of my fantasy series in serialized form on Vella. I also want to draft the next 6 books, so that means books 5 through 10. Book 5 has been a struggle but, maybe, if I give myself some crunch time I can pick and stick to something. Before everyone got sick, I was trying to do some long term planning on the series to try and nail down a better direction for the series but that led to chasing a shiny idea just for book 5. I might flip through my prompt books to see if that will help with some inspiration.

I also want to plan a writing retreat next summer. I might be able to talk Bestie into coming along with me depending on when and where we go. I also would love to visit some of my writing friends. If things go as planned, a bunch of us have been trying to get ideas for a group retreat in the fall of next year. Some people have suggested going around Salem and, yes please! A bunch of fantasy and horror writers in the witchcraft capital of the country? Best trip ever!

Time to have some tea and get back to planning work. Going to probably double down on editing work next week so I can keep on track.

Friday, November 26, 2021

Well, Thanksgiving was yesterday. The chaos of a toddler being on and off sick continues. But, this is actually pretty common according to the pediatrician. We all know, if we have kids, that, while little kids are adorable, they are walking, talking, screaming petri dishes. So, colds are a frequent thing throughout the fall and winter and into the spring. So, I just need to brace myself for that and, from now on, be a little flexible with my goals between October and April. So, once again, I'll be tackling my planner to figure out my work life for 2022 and rearranging things.

But, I did get some writing done this week. Hooray! I finished, mostly, applying the updates to book 2. A LONG overdue project. But, I do have to go back and flesh out a few of the spell casting parts towards the end. I always find it funny that I write fantasy and the spell casting is always the part I struggle with. But, I am going to take my time and do another read through of book 2 before I send it to my friends down the road. There is a lot that needs to be fixed in this one. The word count is low. It is easily 10,000 words less than book 1. If not more. So, I need to improve my detail. I want to see if there are any other plot threads I can weave through. Things like that.

I have been slowly working on notes for the series as a whole. I set up an outline in my document program with a very watered down overview of the books I have drafted, which are books 1 through 4. And, books 1, 2, and 4 have tentative titles. I have notes for overall plot threads that I need to weave through, whether that is the series as a whole or a large portion of the books. I knew I wanted to have a long series. My books are fairly short in comparison to other novels on the market so I felt that a longer series of short books fit best. It is just that, every time I sit down to start another draft, I struggle with the direction I want to take the story. Between remembering what has already happened, what plot points are incomplete that need to be carried over or what can be addressed at another point. At the same time, each story needs its own plot.

For some added inspiration, I borrowed a ton of audio books from the library to my phone. I just did a search for "witch" and clicked on anything with an interesting cover and synopsis. Some was fiction, some was non-fiction. So, I have a lot of content in the coming weeks. I need a new pair of ear buds. My favorite pair died and they were perfect for working at night. I could watch a video or listen to music on my phone or tablet while writing before bed and not worry about waking Hubby. Since my headphones died, I end up staying in my office until nearly midnight. My headset that I use for my computer is connected by USB and that is not compatible with my phone or tablet.

As much as I want to keep going marking up books 3 and 4 drafts, I do need to go back to book 1 and actually look at the feedback my friends sent me. I also need to book time with the editor. If I can't reserve February/March, I may need to move my projected publication date to Vella for book 1 from May to another time in the year. Also, need to figure out a cover design for that book and do whatever else that a book launch requires, even for serial form.

The next couple weeks will be emotional draining so, while I am trying to do my best, I am not going to get too overly upset if I can't get a ton done other than my top 3 or 4 goals. And then a refresh start in 2022!

Friday, December 17, 2021

So, earlier this year, I had started a series on my YouTube channel where I invited other creators on to chat about their work. It went until... March? And then I was having a hard time coordinating with people and then life got crazy so it got put on hold. I want to bring it back in the coming year so I've started reaching out again to people might be interested. And, on a long shot, I emailed one of my favorite D&D channels and the creators of another channel that I love. They do videos about history and writing and literature and mythology.

I hit send and then began to freak out. What if they said no? What if they just ignored me? I might be able to handle that because I don't even have 200 subscribers yet. I don't have a large, regularly active platform. Creators with hundreds of thousands of viewers aren't going to pay attention to my teeny corner of the Web.

And then, I thought, "Ooh, crap. What if they say yes? I have to make sure my office is immaculate and perfectly decorated.

I have to make sure my interview questions are per-fec-tion! Why did I email them? Why did I put so much pressure on myself?" Ah, the joys of anxiety.

So I freaked out to my friends and they were wonderful and encouraging so, if these people do say yes, I could have some fun. And, incentive to fix up my office a bit more. I have been thinking about getting a fun backdrop tapestry to hang... somehow.

December is half over. How? How is Christmas next weekend? How is 2022 less than 2 weeks away? At the same time, it's like "Thank God this is almost over!" The past 5 months have been one chaotic mess after another. And I'm ready to start new. I want to look forward to something new and maybe some better news about the Plague? Like... say, a vaccine for kids under 5?

For the rest of the month and into January, I'll be looking over the feedback I've received from friends and do one more round of self edits before I finalize plans with the editor. I definitely want to get book 1 up in serial format before I plan a big, compiled release. Once book 1 is up in serial, I can work on 2 and beyond and get those up. Treating that platform as a sort of soft launch. And then I can take some time and correctly format, get an exciting cover, and all the other things for a full book release.

I say all this as we make plans to begin toilet training Peanut. She could start transitional preschool as early as May right after her birthday. So, starting in February, we'll be meeting with the school district to get that ball rolling. Maybe for her birthday, we'll shift her from the crib to a "big kid bed" as well. My little girl is growing up so fast!

It's so funny when I look on Facebook and the memories pop up. Today was from last year when she learned the word "Wow!" Every time we turned on the Christmas lights, she'd crawl over as fast as her little arms and legs would move and just stare in awe whispering "Wow!" Now, we have a little ritual. She points to the tree and says "La" for "lights." I go to the switch. "Ready... set..." "Go!" she finishes. And then dances and cheers when I flip the lights on.

Last night, we met with my sister and her kids in the town square of the town we grew up in to see their light display. Everything was a wonder for the kids. They tried to climb into Santa's sleigh, pet the lambs at the Nativity set, and danced on the gazebo where Christmas songs played on a speaker. Sunday, we're going to my mom's to make cookies and then, since it gets dark around 5PM, we'll go drive around looking at lights. It'll be my reward for spending Saturday and Sunday cleaning my office some more.

I've been playing a lot of Sims 4 lately. Until I can coordinate with Bestie so she can teach my how to play D&D, I needed another outlet of escape besides writing and reading where I can pretend the issues of the world aren't a thing for a few hours. And, I have the Realm of Magic pack which is really fun to play with. In the game I'm playing to livestream, my character just bought a big house and adopted a daughter. I put in a gorgeous garden and spent over an hour decorating all the rooms. Yes, I did cheat because my Sim is also a freelance writer. But, I wanted to move her story along a bit more so it was exciting for people to watch. I might treat myself to another expansion pack someday to change things up. Just don't know when that will be since I have some other work related upgrades to work on.

I must be off and get some more things done. So much to do, and seemingly never enough time to do it.

Tuesday, January 4, 2022

It's been a year since I started writing this thing. Wow!

Happy New Year! We made it through another plague filled Christmas but this time, at least, we were able to see family in person and not through a tablet screen. So, points for improvement?

Also, a word of warning, this entry is going to be all over the place. I should be asleep But, Bestie decided to tag me in an old post from the Great Lakes Medieval Faire Facebook group about auditions so now I am trying to tweak one of my table top roleplay characters and decide if I should audition. Because hyper-fixation is the name of the game inside my brain! I've been already getting ideas to bring this character to life because we want to go to another fair out of state the weekend of my birthday. But, I don't think I can try out. They would need to accommodate my work schedule. Boss Lady is wonderfully flexible but doubtful she'll let me take off an entire summer. Also, between rehearsals starting in May and then the fair itself, that takes me away from my family every weekend all summer. So, instead, maybe I'll spring for a season pass and see how many times I can get there as an attendee this summer. Maybe I can get Hubby to come along with Peanut. But, there was a lot we didn't get to see in one weekend last year so having the time to take my time and see more would be great. And, it would pay for itself in 2 weekends.

I need to get back to my self edits so I can plan things with my editor. Big goal for this year is release book 1 this year! I am thinking summer or fall.

I took the last couple months to do whatever because my brain was being a jerk: between stress and grief and then it had to go throw Impostor Syndrome on top of it. But, tomorrow, I'm going to start jumping back into it. I am going to look at the feedback I've received, do one last monster self edit, and then contact the editor to book our time. This period of self editing will make sure I am able to pay them as well.

Next, I need to figure out how my book cover will look. I might ask some friends for ideas on where to look and see what I can afford. And then see who does the best work in my budget.

I did get a new book about self publishing as a Christmas gift so I will be looking over that as well.

Pretty exciting finally looking at being at this point. It's definitely a dream come true. If everything goes according to plan, I may have the book out in time for the arts festival in the town I grew up in. It's in the fall so I think I can pull it off.

I definitely will look into events at the library as well. They're slowly starting in person events again. Yay! I miss going to library events so much.

Despite being weird, I think we did have a nice Christmas. The kids had fun and that was top priority. Grandmas went all out on goodies for them. Peanut learned how fun it was to rip wrapping paper. So much so that, when we went to my in-laws on New Years Day for dinner and gift exchange, she wanted to help everyone else with theirs. It was the cutest.

Peanut has also learned more words. Or at least she can say them enough that we know what she is trying to say. Every day, she points to the tree and says "Li" (sounds like lie) for lights. I'll count "one, two..." "'Reee!" she'll finish and I flip the switch. I wasn't sure of the sign for lunch so we just sign the letter L and she says "luh" when I ask her if she wants lunch. She almost completely says "bread." That is a favorite nighttime snack. Yep. Just a slice of white bread. Or Italian if we have it. Such a carbivore. And, "Ball" is a recent and frequent word, too.

So, between speech and daycare and continued work at home, she's made massive improvements. And, when she starts preschool, it will get even better and I'm so happy and proud of her.

I had a lovely chat with a friend as 2021 closed. I didn't realize the heavy cloud on my mind from the last 5 months or so. It got so bad that I couldn't see the good things from the year. Which is crazy because I wrote about quite a bit of them in this book! But, then G mentioned them and I was like, "Oh yeah! It wasn't all bad after all." So, I am making more of a point this year to document good memories. I have a set spot in my planner and even found a 5 year memory book to write a few lines each day. Then, when I am in one of those clouds, I can grab the book and look back. It won't eliminate the cloud but maybe make it lighter. Is this making sense or do I need to go to bed?

I mean, yes. I do. It's nearly midnight. So, before another tangent is started, happy new year to all, and to all a good night!

Sunday, January 9, 2022

Good morning dear people,

How was the first week of your year? Mine was surprisingly productive. I worked up the courage to read the extensive feedback report a friend wrote up. And, she only read half the book. Half! But, it was really good and insightful and I suddenly had all the ideas! Basically, my first half drags and there is more focus on the romantic subplot than the magic. I also need to refine my magic system rules.

Now, saying this also makes me realize that book 2-4 will need lots of work to keep everything consistent but I'll worry about that later. Focusing on my publishing target first and then I can move forward in the series.

I already like what I have done so far. I picked up on things that she didn't. But, that's because there are details I know like exact dates and I saw some major plot holes regarding the timeline. But, they're easily fixable.

I have a little added inspiration on my desk at home to help me when the Imp (What my friend MM calls Imposter

Syndrome) tells me I suck. Something I needed before I tackled this feedback and revision.

I started collecting oracle and tarot decks last year. Mostly because they're pretty. And then a writing friend we'll call KL has a tarot based timer system for her productivity sprints. There is one deck that I love called the Divine Feminine deck. The artwork is absolutely gorgeous. It's by Meggan Watterson and the artist is Lisbeth Cheever-Gessamen. I love that it features various historical and mythical figures like Joan of Arc, Sappho, assorted goddesses, and Pope Joan, who may not have existed but her story is still fascinating. I was feeling really anxious about this feedback so I decided to draw a card and see if it offered any motivation. When I shuffled, one jumped out. Brigid, an Irish goddess. Now, I was raised Catholic. But, I enjoy drawing inspiration from other beliefs. And, I have some Irish ancestry, I believe. So, I decided to see what the card description had to say. In the booklet that comes with the deck, it talked about Brigid being the goddess of light and guiding you from darkness into light. Shifting toward something new and better. And, it is exactly what I needed to hear after the past 2 years. There is hope!

And, it also fits with my theme I am trying for the year. A bunch of writers have joined together to say we are not going to let things hold us back from what we want anymore. At least not things in our control. MM, whom I mentioned earlier, started it last year. She wrote a ton of words and published, I think, 10 books! In a single year! After battling some severe health issues. That's so kick ass amazing!

Now, I will be the first to admit. I am my biggest barrier. I am a chronic procrastinator. My brain is filled with all of the guilt. Mom guilt, self care guilt. You know. "Why are you taking a nap? Get up and do that hustle!" Or "Why are you writing? You are missing all the important things with your child!" And then I get mad at myself when I don't reach my goals. So, it's time to change that this year. I will not let myself be held back anymore. I have wanted to be published since I can remember. I am going to show my little one what hard work can accomplish.

Alright, I got my thoughts out for the day. I need to review my planner tasks for the week and then I can get to writing.

Sunday, January 23, 2022

We have a week(ish) left in January. Where did the time go? I have been getting some edits done but I have also been working on a crochet project to go with my renaissance fair costume for a trip I am planning in May. My best friend and I are going to a small fair the weekend of my birthday. So, I have been on a very strict spending ban to save up, unless it's a very important business expense.

Like the editor. Because that's happening soon. Eek!

I reached out to the editor to let them know I would be booking a time with them in early February to do a full developmental edit. So I will be one step closer to being ready for release! Then I'm going to make a list of other author friends who do prep work like formatting and cover design. I want to support people I know if I can before looking elsewhere. There are several people who are multi-talented in my friend group. I just have to figure out who fits in my budget and what their time frame is. I have an idea of an image I would like on the cover but I do not have the ability to pull it off myself. I also want all my covers to coordinate so that's another thing to consider.

Also, as of last night, I have another story idea. I stayed up way too late brainstorming but I regret nothing!

It all started when I decided to create a character for Dungeons and Dragons. Bestie has been begging me to come play. It's just that coordinating that is easier said than done. Between my job and juggling appointments for Peanut, and she has 4 kids all in activities, life is busy. But, I had this idea for a character and I started playing around. Then, I thought this character would be fun to play next time I go to a renaissance fair so I started fleshing out her story and figuring out my costume.

Then a light bulb turned on.

What if I took a little time each day and wrote out a story using this character? It would be a change of pace and, when I am stuck on a project, it helps to work on something else for fun to refill the creative well. I used to do it with fan fiction all the time. And maybe there can be crossover between the two stories. (Yes, it will probably be a series because that is how my brain works. I start with one story and then I must lose myself in the world and write all the things.) Last night, and a bit today, I worked on the character and her family. I did a bit of world building in a notebook. This week I will make copies of the series bible worksheets I found for the contemporary series and I'll also create everything on World Anvil so it's saved digitally. If I get artsy, I may attempt a map. This can be my reward project. When I complete the tasks for the contemporary fantasy, I'll switch to work on the other one. All of the stories! Yes, please.

I think this will be a serialized story. If I release it that way, it will motivate me to keep working on it instead of getting distracted and moving on before it's done.

With that in mind, I think 2022 will be a lot of fun. It was a slow start but I see big things ahead. And I'm excited to continue sharing the journey.

Sunday, January 30, 2022

Lots of things are happening as we're ending January and heading into February! We're starting potty training for little Peanut. She's not big on changes to her routine so it will be a fight at first. But, like most things, she'll eventually catch on and take to it like a champ. So, I will probably be limiting my work time so that can be my focus for a while.

We also have a video meeting with her speech therapy and the school district this week. We're starting preparations for preschool, which could start as early as May. Another big step for my little girl. But, it's an exciting one. She's done really well in daycare. I think she'll thrive in preschool.

I officially sent book 1 of my modern fantasy series to the editor! I finished up all my self edits today and emailed the document. It'll take about a month for him to read it and work on all his notes and then we'll do a video call to go over his report and suggestions. I also have a mock-up cover that I am going to send to a friend and ask them if they can make it better for the actual cover. I have an idea in my head of what I want. Executing that... I definitely lack the skill for it. But, I know many people very skilled in cover design that can either offer suggestions or I could eventually hire to completely revamp. And then I'll be on track for my possible late summer/early fall goal to publish! What even?

But, first, I am going to take some time and work on the other project I've been calling the D&D Plot Bunny. It was started with an idea for a character I made for when I am eventually able to play D&D with my bestie and her family. I started getting more ideas for her back story and I could not get it out of my head. It was distracting me from editing! So, once I got the manuscript emailed for the first series, I started outlining this one. And I am having so much fun.

I already have a prologue and nearly 2 chapters outlined. And, my plan is to try to reach the midpoint by the end of the week. I've also been going through my various prompt books to get ideas for other stories once this one is done. Because, yes, this will be another series. It's kinda how my brain works. I get an idea and then I must write all of the things!

I have never written a fantastical story quite like this. For nearly 10 years, the world I've been writing in has been close to our ordinary world. Like, sure, I made up the town but it is basically our modern world with witches. So, to be able to make up a whole new world with its own culture and a whole pantheon is an entirely different experience for me. It's been fun, though. I've spent hours on World Anvil working on world building. I also have a dedicated notebook for when I'm on the go or in bed writing before I sleep at night. I have pages for a story bible that I need to make copies of at the library this week, one day after I take Peanut to daycare. I have some binders that I'm not using to keep all the pages together and plenty of loose leaf for additional notes. This format has worked for the modern series and I'm pretty sure I can adapt it for this more medieval style world.

If all goes well, I can get it written, revised, and up in a serial format sometime in the spring. I hope people enjoy it. I'm laying into the tropes to get as wild and crazy as possible. I've been looking up prompts in the books I have to get new ideas for future stories in this world. And, of course, using Fantasy Name Generator to come up with names for things. Just, in some categories, you really have to search to make sure the name selected doesn't look like a cat walked on your keyboard. I like to have things to be pronounceable.

This is definitely going to be a fun project for me. Not like the other one isn't fun. The modern fantasy series has been my book baby for the past 8 years. But, this new one is so different from what I'm used to. It'll be a nice change of pace. I've also never juggled two projects before so that will be interesting and a challenge.

I better get back to writing. And, with two projects to juggle, updates may be more frequent now. Woohoo!

Thursday, February 3, 2022

It's already been a busy week. Peanut had her usual appointments and daycare this week. Yesterday Hubby and I had a Zoom meeting with one of the organizations we work with for Peanut's speech therapy and the local school district to start talking about preschool prep this fall and today we started potty training!

Today, we are hunkering down inside because it is snowing like mad and I do not want to be on the road. Hubby is even working from home today, which has been unusual, but his office is in the basement so he's able to focus on what he needs to do.

I just laid Peanut down for quiet time and I am ready to get to work on the "D&D Plot Bunny" story. I finished outlining chapter 3 this morning before I got Peanut up for breakfast. I also started working on writing out the chapters that I have already outline. So far I'm halfway through chapter 2. I've actually changed a lot of things from the original outline already but it'll be better for it. I was kind of distracted when I was outlining over the weekend in my little notebook because I was at Bestie's house and it's just chaos there.

I'm having so much fun with this story. I know I keep saying this but it's true. I've been bouncing between outlining and world building. Every time I write about a new character or a new feature of the world, I make a note of it in my binder and then create a World Anvil article to flesh out later so I'm keeping up on all my information. Once I get to the midpoint, I'll probably start sharing with a few close friends and get their feedback. I have the document set up for 30 chapters. Could be less, could be more. That all remains to be seen, of course.

I created a character last night that I know will be a lot of fun to write about. Not going to say much about it other than they are super sassy and I am in love. I almost grabbed my tablet and pulled up my D&D app to make a character sheet for them for when I actually get a chance to play with people, whenever that may be. But, that could also count as a distraction when it comes to writing. Or, that information can be used in their character profile and worked into the story so it could count as world building?

I've been tossing around title names as well for this story. If all goes as planned, I could start releasing it serially by the end of the month or early March. Since my modern fantasy book will be with the editor for close to a month, I have time to focus on the Plot Bunny. Which works out since that is all I want to work on right now.

I have not had an all consuming need to focus on a story in a long time. I've enjoyed the 4 stories I've written for the modern fantasy but it hasn't distracted me from life like this one has been. I even downloaded Google Docs on my phone so I can work on the first draft when I'm not in my office. I try not to do that. I took that app off my phone for a reason so I could better devote to family time. So, fighting this desire to write has been a big struggle for me.

Last time I had a feeling to constantly work on a story like this was in 2013 when I did NaNoWriMo seriously for the first time. I kept a daily vlog- that's how I started my YouTube channel. But, for a variety of reasons, I never finished. One of those reasons being I lost the story but that's a tale or another time. I worked retail at the time and I kept a little notebook on me at all times to write on my breaks and at every chance I had.

So, enough talk about it. I'm off to work on this story more. Don't think I am going to reach my goal of hitting halfway this week so maybe next week that can happen. We'll see how much progress I can make over the weekend.

Wednesday, February 16, 2022

So, I have so many thoughts that I have to share and I need to share all of my excitement from the past couple hours.

I've been making (slow) progress on D&D Plot Bunny. I was bouncing between outlining and drafting. I started outlining chapter 7 this morning. If I can get at least a chapter per day on the outline, I could finish it before the end of the month, finish the first draft in the first half of March, and first round of edits done by the end of March.

From now on, I'm calling my contemporary series The Witches Series so there is no more confusion. So, for that series, I am spending the rest of the month making notes for each chapter. I talked with the editor today for over an hour and I had SO many thoughts and ideas. The light bulbs in my brain were going off with revelations and epiphanies and all of the twists and turns t improve the story. And, not just book 1. These are story beats that will carry over into future books. So, once I finish the notes for book 1, I might dive into books

2-4 and just make notes before all of the things leave my brain.

But, I could not believe this meeting. First, I was late. He texted me while I was on the way to work to get tested for the plague. And then I had stopped to get lunch. When I told him how long it would take to get home, I hit every red light on the way home and then my computer was sooooooo sllloooooooow firing up! In all, it made me about 15 minutes late. But, he was cool with it and we got right down to it.

And, I knew J was thorough. Other friends have told me who has used his services. Be ready for all the ideas. But, holy bologna! He pointed out things I never considered! And I've been working on this for almost 8 years. And I've done at least 1 complete overhaul rewrite. But, I guess, it's true what they say about the benefit of outside feedback on your writing. You're too close to your work so that you don't catch the issues.

I am really looking forward to working on this, though. It's renewed my enthusiasm for the series that I haven't had in many months. It was part of the reason I jumped into Plot Bunny. My brain needed a shift for a while. But, now I have all of these ideas for Witches. I know I will be up very late tonight working on it. I have a notebook specifically dedicated to that book. And, I always print my drafts so I can write all over the pages and highlight. These drafts are in Technicolor by the time I'm done.

I also might see if Bestie is free to have a brainstorm session with me to help work things out further. She and I used to write together all the time. She is still my go-to sounding board when I have ideas and she is a master at character creation. Part of why she enjoys D&D so much.

And, I love Plot Bunny. I have so many ideas for this story, the world as a whole, and then future stories. My World Anvil page is going to be massive once I fill in all the info for this world. Between the pantheon, which is extensive, different religions, types of magic users, the various geographical and man-made landmarks. I have a binder full of paper that I have loose notes written on for each thing. And then I'll go in and turn those notes into a coherent article for people to read. It'll also be in one spot for my own reference as well.

So, yeah. I'm going to get to work! I have to finish outlining chapter 7 in Plot Bunny and then I will jump into Witches and add to J's notes. Excited to see where this goes!

In my theme of "Do all the things!" this year, you may see 2 books out this year. Wait and see!

Monday, February 28, 2022

Well, here we are at the end of another month. How? What? Where is the time going? Does anyone else feel like the time goes by faster when you're not doing anything? Like, past 2 years now, with the restrictions in place for the Plague and being cautious, time seems to just zoom by.

Although, I have plans for this spring and summer! Trips to the zoo, the beach, maybe some of the many museums around here. I think Peanut would really enjoy those new experiences. Down by the art museum, there are cherry blossoms by a little reflecting pool and it is gorgeous when they are in bloom. I might need to get a larger memory card for my camera and my phone for all the photos and videos I plan on taking.

Today I had a meeting with the school district psychologist to schedule the evaluation for Peanut so we can start planning her transition to preschool in the fall. So, that's exciting and unbelievable in a way. Three years have really flown by.

While, there were some times when that time felt like it would never end while I was going through it. And then I look back and go, "Wow! That was that long ago?" But, I like this program that they do where they work with kids with developmental delays and really pull in all the resources they can to help catch them up. I think it is going to help a lot. Just since September when we started daycare, her vocabulary has exploded and she's learning to play around other children. Her mood has been better. Her ability to self soothe when she's upset has improved. But, there's still a bit of help she needs to be more expressive in her communication.

We also had our pastor and a friend of my dad's over for dinner last night to plan her reception to the parish. We had her baptized at home so this is finishing the everything actually in Church. So, I made a big dinner and we sat and talked and planned a tentative date... that I'll already have to change because it's a work weekend. Note to self: When planning things, have your planner nearby to verify the things! Of course, Peanut stole the show. She ran around and danced and sang. And then, she ran to the living room window and waved and blew kisses when everyone left. The meal was great. I tried to replicate my dad's lasagna (minus mushrooms in the filling because gross) and everyone said he would have been proud.

Since we were so focused on tidying the house for company, I did not get much writing done. I restarted my outline for Plot Bunny. For right now, I have things broken down by what happens in each location in my world and how long my little band is in each place. I even drew a little map just to have a kind of idea of where things are. It's not to scale or anything. But, it gives me a general idea of where things are. Once I am able, I'd like to find some map making software, like something to do with tabletop gaming, and plan something out. And then I'll be able to share the images on social media with everyone. I have plans for future stories thanks to a world building journal I found at a bookstore with a ton of prompts that got the wheels turning again. I just need to finish this one first before I move on!

If I can get the Plot Bunny story up by sometime in May, I'd be a very happy camper. I am not setting anything in stone until I am closer to being done. I always intended for that to be serialized. I may do a compiled release down the road, if my readership is good and I have more stories in the series. But, for right now, it will only be serialized.

I think this new outline method will work out. I got maybe 1/3 done just on Wednesday and then printed it out to write the rest by hand. And, I picked up a pack of loose leaf paper so I can write up all my notes on the pantheon and magic system and different locations in this country I made up. I'm trying to balance the writing and world building so I don't get sucked into one thing or the other. I have never gone so in depth on a world like this. My "Witches" series is more modern. I mean, I planned out the town. But, this is a whole country with a pantheon of deities and a royal family and a government. Building it from scratch. And, it might get bigger for future stories. This first story is going to be my main character's call to a life as an adventurer and then I can just go from there and get crazy. I'm so excited to continue to get into it.

I also consulted a friend who writes horror to get her opinion on a magical item in the story. I wanted to make sure I captured how bad this thing is and it's the mission of my characters to destroy it or lots of bad happens to the world. She loved it! So that got me even more pumped to keep working.

It's time to get back to work.

Sunday, March 6, 2022

Well, draft 1 of the Plot Bunny outline is done and I sent it to 3 friends to get suggestions for improvements. I am also going to spend some of tonight and this week where I can on "series bible" notes so I can have my world building more consistent. This is going to be a massive tale so I need all of the notes I can to keep everything in my head.

Since I've been so busy with Plot Bunny, I haven't touched Witches in a while. Not since I went through it after my developmental edit. But, Plot Bunny has kinda been taking over my brain. I have had dreams about the possibilities for this story. Only remembering glimpses because that's how my brain works. But, I think a lot can come from it. So, I've been hyper focused on trying to knock it out and plan the next one.

I am happy to have at least this rickety skeleton of a story down. Hopefully, with feedback and the world building, the rest of the layers will develop to help make the story more cohesive. And then it should be much easier to write.

I committed to participating in Camp NaNoWriMo in April. I only set my goal for 20,000 words. My outline is currently about 5,000 words. So, if the first draft is at least 4 times that, I think it's tremendous progress. I haven't done Camp in a long time. I like it because it's more relaxed compared to the big National Novel Writing Month in November. At least, during Camp, you can pick your word count. And that's great if you want to write but have a demanding job or family obligations. Or, if you just don't write novels.

I am going to spend some time at the library tomorrow printing off some worksheets that I have saved over time to give me a hand with my info tracking. I think that will be my focus tomorrow for a couple hours. I'll make some general notes in my binder today when I return home from work. Then, tomorrow, after I drop off Peanut to daycare, I will head to the library and print off what I need to print. Then, I need to run up to work to get tested and finally I'll come home to prepare for an interview I am recording! Another writer invited me to take part in an authortube series highlighting smaller channels, which is great. I have been trying to get more content on YouTube so this will be a motivational boost.

My week is a little thrown off. Peanut has something going on every day this week. Monday and Friday is daycare. Wednesday, she has an ophthalmology appointment, and her regular therapy sessions on Tuesday and Thursday. That is a lot going on so we're going to try and make the weekend a bit more chill to make up for it.

Yesterday, after work, I joined a couple friends for a Self Care Saturday livestream. We chatted about anything and everything. My friend had sent me a face mask in a goodie box so we did the face masks, which I had never used before. I painted my nails a pale purple color that I had in my stash. Then, we fired up some video games to close out the night. I did not go to bed until almost 1 a.m. so getting up this morning was a bit of a slog but I have no regrets. We want to try and make it a regular thing. I may look for some more masks because it felt really good.

Friday, March 11, 2022

Ever have a driving need to get something accomplished but you also feel like absolute crap? That's been me the past 3 days. My back has been tight and aching, it hurts to move, but I have so many ideas in my head that I am determined to push through the pain and do all the things I need to do.

I'm used to pain flares. Comes with having a chronic pain condition. It doesn't help that I have not taken my medication in a couple weeks. We received a bill for the full, astronomical cost and I didn't want to reorder it. Long story short, after a couple stressful hours on the phone, got things taken care of and I can reorder things. I do, though, think I am going to talk to my doctor about another option that doesn't cause so much stress to the checkbook. I made an appointment for later this month.

But, I can't afford to stay in bed and sleep the pain away. Since Hubby works all day, I have to do all the things for Peanut. She has had appointments almost every day this week bookended by daycare. And I have to still go get tested twice a week for the part time job. (We almost made it a whole 3 days out of outbreak status at the end of February but then the number of cases in the county went up) So, I have been taking advantage of nap times and the daycare days with a bottle of ibuprofen nearby in case I absolutely need it.

I am still hyper focused on the Plot Bunny story. I went to the library on Monday and printed off a bunch of worksheets to help with world building. I managed to find an old binder and some unused dividers and made the beginnings of a story bible. I spent Monday and Tuesday working on the pantheon in this story's world. It's quite extensive and I don't know if I'll use all of them but there are at least 2 that play a large role in the first book.

On Wednesday, I started playing around with ideas for an outline for the second book in the series. I was looking through prompts trying to come up with ideas and I found a lot of fantasy prompts that dealt with royalty. And then I had a light bulb moment. (I love those. I get so giddy when the brain just goes "Oooh! I know how to fix the thing!") I started scribbling away and didn't get to bed until almost midnight. Yesterday, after I laid Peanut down for her nap, I decided to not wait until April and started the first draft of book 1 of the Plot Bunny series. I figured it would help outline book 2 if I an flesh out the details of book 1. I didn't want to wait until I received feedback from my friends. I can always make changes in edits.

Despite the amount of pain I was in, I wrote over 2100 words in 3 hours. And then I couldn't take sitting in my office chair anymore so I spent the evening with Hubby and Peanut and went back to work after she was in bed.

Since she's going to daycare today, I'm hoping to at least double what I wrote yesterday when I get home from testing at work. I have some laundry to do so that will force me to get up once in a while, which should help my back from getting too tight. I'll also reorder my medication today as well.

Tomorrow, we're sending Peanut to my in-laws overnight and going out to see Bestie and her family. It's her younger son's birthday and they're hosting a game night, so I might be able to play my first D&D campaign! I'll make sure to have a notebook on hand in case I get some more ideas for Plot Bunny.

Well, time to get some work done before I have to get Peanut out of bed. We'll see how I do today.

Monday, March 21, 2022

Well, last week... happened. I had such high hopes for getting things done. I finished the Plot Bunny first book outline, started a little bit of the sequel, and even started the rough draft. I made great progress. Four and a half chapters in two days, not too shabby. And then it all came to a screeching halt.

Wednesday, Peanut was at daycare as per usual and I was working away. I had to go to work and get tested for the Rona and, as I was ready to head out the door, I received a text saying we were out of outbreak status. Cool! Fully vaccinated people don't have to go get tested. And, at $4+ per gallon, that's great news. I went and treated myself to lunch and went back to work. 2 hours later, another message to disregard the first. So, I had to stop, drive 45 minutes to work, get the test (which took time because everyone was scrambling now) and drive 45 minutes home. Nearly 2 hours I could have spent maintaining the good momentum gone. When I got home, I lost all desire to write so I worked on world building just to say I was productive. And, I've been doing that ever since.

I have 2 giant binders stuffed with paper and I am slowly filling in information in various categories. I'm handwriting everything because my printer isn't set up and I don't have ink or paper even if it was. I've shared pictures on my crowdfunding page and talked about my setup. That was a lot of fun to write about. Eventually, I'll type it up and make the format all pretty.

A table top gamer I follow in Australia recommended a YouTube channel with a series about drawing maps. I spent most of today sketching out the island and marking out cities, rivers, and major roads. When I can find room in my budget, I want to sign up for a map making platform of some kind to fancy it up. I'd love a poster of this world on my wall and to have it available for readers to buy eventually. And, if I release this story in a non-serialized format, I could have the art in the book.

My calendar has been full of appointments. Between Peanut's therapy and doctor appointments and preschool prep, my appointments and work schedule, hubby's appointments and work schedule, and events with family and friends, it's amazing that I have found time to work when I have. It usually means late nights and early mornings but worth it. I do need to schedule my tasks a little better so I can complete other projects instead of hyper-fixating on one. Like,, mornings could be spent working on "Witches" (my contemporary fantasy) Afternoon could be Plot Bunny work, and evenings while I'm chatting with friends and watching them play games in a chat server, I could work on administrative tasks.

But, it's spring now so that's nice. (Technically. The calendar says spring now. Will the weather show that? Meh... it's northeast Ohio.) I've bee opening all of the windows when the thermometer is above 50 degrees. I'm considering taking Peanut to the park one day next week and see if my mom wants to go on a little adventure with us.

I also have about a month and a half to plan birthday stuffs for Peanut. I have to consider weather and my work schedule for anything with extended family and friends. As someone with a May birthday as well, I know how hit and miss weather can be. Many a parties were planned well into June to have warmer, sunnier days. And then everyone can be outside. Day of, we'll probably have my mom and in-laws over for dinner and cake. It'll be a fun time. And then another day can be my bestie and her family, my sister and her family, and maybe some aunts and uncles.

It's late so time for bed. Ready to get the things done this week. And I'm going to a writing conference at the library on Saturday. I'll talk about that after it happens.

Friday, March 25, 2022

Ever have a day, or a series of days where nothing seems to go right? And, then you get that nasty little Imposter Syndrome in your head, or what my friend, MM, just call "The Imp," pointing out all your flaws and exaggerating things to make everything seem like your fault? And, it turns the anxiety up to 15 so even the slightest thing is cause for overwhelm and you just want to hide in bed?

No? Just me? Well, aren't you lucky if that's the case.

But, that's been my head the past 2 days. It started yesterday when Peanut made it very clear in her way she did not want to be at Speech Therapy. So, we had to cut the session short. (Plus side, if I had to find one, we won't be billed for it at least.) We had lunch and had a pretty chill rest of the day aside from Hubby fighting off a cold. I helped my friend CE's game stream, which is always loads of fun, and I thought everything was better.

And, today was okay until I went to work. We had some higher ups coming in to do a check of things so everyone was on edge. We had nonstop people between visitors and shift change the whole first half of my shift so I felt like I couldn't breathe for 3 hours. Also, a new rule not allowing us to leave the desk unattended so I couldn't go to the cafeteria and warm my soup cup that I brought for dinner. (I only would have been gone for 5 minutes but I did not want to get in trouble. I'll have to come up with something else in future. May have to dig out my small cooler to pack things next time I work a Friday night) All the stress! I was going to order dinner instead but the only thing that looked appetizing had shrimp and/or bacon. Neither of which are allowed as they adhere to Jewish Kosher practices. I did have snacks, though, so I didn't have to worry about my blood sugar tanking or something like that. But, I had a major headache.

So, I decided I wanted a self care night. I came home and Peanut was already in bed so I chatted with Hubby for a bit. And then I took a shower and treated myself to an old favorite movie and a pint of ice cream. Oh, and a watermelon face mask. It was lovely and I felt much more relaxed.

Tomorrow, I am going to the Western Reserve Writers Conference at the library. I will definitely write about it in the near future. It's an all day event with speakers and a book sale. I've gone a few times and it's always so fascinating. I'm going to try and focus on business lectures since this is my year to publish. That's pretty important to learn. And, I'll definitely check out the books on sale. I will have to have some restraint since I'm still trying to pay down my credit card for my trip in September but I'm always looking for more craft books.

On Sunday, back to writing. I have a lot to work on if I want to serialize Plot Bunny this summer and get "Witches" out in the fall sometime. I'm making slow progress on Plot Bunny. About 5 1/2 chapters in and a partial outline of book 2. I think I can get these written and up quickly. Still trying to juggle everything.

Alright, this introvert needs to rest up for all the "peopleing" tomorrow. Good night, all!

Sunday, March 27, 2022

Sunday, March 27, 2022

I was going to write about the writers conference when I got home last night. I had all of the thoughts as I was driving home. So many ideas I needed to sort out and put into place to improve my work and my business... and then I came home and remembered I am an introvert and how much being around crowds exhausts me. So, I had dinner and joined my friends on a livestream for a Self Care night and then crashed in bed.

But, I'm here now, at my desk. Refreshed and fueled by caffeine. I enjoyed myself a lot at the conference. If I could have one criticism, it is very traditional publishing focused. A lot about contracts and how to get an agent and how to write for industry standards. And that's great. I'm not knocking anyone who wants to publish that way. But, it doesn't do much good for self-published writers like I want to be. I did find some talks that were helpful, though, and I'll keep an eye out on the library event calendar for something more focused on the direction I want to take.

So, the first talk I attended was called "What Authors Should Know About the Law: Publishing Law 101." I did get some great notes from this talk and I plan on buying the presenter's book down the road. She talked about Copyright law, what is defamation, the difference between copyright and trademarks. I think I took 3 pages of notes and it wasn't enough to catch all of what she said.

The second set of talks, I was torn between two. There was one on editing and one on creating diverse characters. I chose the editing one since that will be my focus on Plot Bunny very soon. But, the presenter for the character talk does a lot at the library so I know I'll catch her again at some point.

Again, I couldn't write fast enough for all of the notes I took. A lot of good tips on developing a process to self edit your work. And, she didn't even get into getting outside feedback. That could have been another hour long presentation.

After that talk, everyone broke for lunch. One of a few times the library bent the rules about allowing food. I grabbed a sandwich and chatted with a couple other attendees.

After lunch, there was a "First Page Critique" session. People could submit their first page of a WIP, the Writers Center Librarian read it outloud (not saying the author's name) and some of the day's speakers would comment on it. They were really critical for a lot of the submissions. I'd almost say nit-picky which is why I've never submitted anything.

The final set of talks was a choice between 1) Understanding the traditional publishing world: types of houses, understanding contracts, that kind of thing, 2) Writing about being from Ohio- especially focused toward non-fiction and memoir writers, and 3) Writing short stories. I chose the last one and I'm glad I did. The presenter was so entertaining. I actually ended up following her on Twitter. And, while I didn't take notes when she talked about where to submit those stories, I did get some good tips on story structure that can be applied whether you're writing 1000 words or 100,000 words.

For the last half hour, everyone came back to the main event room for door prizes and book signings. One of the local bookstores had set up a table so I did pick up a couple books, but not as many as I would have liked. I had to remember about my trip coming up so that, sadly, kept me from getting all the books. I did win one, too! My ticket was pulled for the door prize and I picked out a book by Adam Savage, who is one of the Mythbusters. If I wasn't so tired when I came home, I would have started reading right away. Maybe I'll see if there's an audiobook version.

So, that was my experience at the Western Reserve Writers Conference. First library event in 2 years and I could tell everyone there was excited for it. I am checking out the website all the time for more events. I just have to figure out how to fit them into my schedule.

I've considered going back to school and taking some business classes at the community college but that's not in my budget right now. But, I have several friends who are very knowledgeable of that end of the industry so I can always ask them for advice when needed.

Today's focus as we get into the afternoon is to try and finish at least chapter 6 of Plot Bunny. And, I might go back to the start and tweak a few things. I got some ideas on how to better start the first chapter. And, it's Sunday Fun Day later on my friend CE's chat server so I can always read things out loud to get feedback on what I have so far.

If I can bust this draft out by the middle of April, I can spend the rest of the month editing. May can be feedback and more revisions. As much as I'd like to release a serial version in May, it might have to be June. But, that's okay. It gives me a little extra time to polish it... and come up with a real title. Once it's all scheduled, I can concentrate on book 2, which already has a partial outline. And, I know I'll get more inspiration in September at the Renaissance fest. I plan on bringing a notebook with me to write down all the things.

My costume is slowly coming together for that trip! I bought 2 flowy skirts I plan on wearing as a kind of petticoat. I showed Hubby the other dress I want and asked him to get it for my birthday. (Fingers crossed it arrives in time for the festival. It should if he orders it in May)

I'm going to order a back brace to help with walking and Peanut and I are going to start walking as much as possible so I can build up my endurance. Even if it's just starting with looping the cul-de-sac and working my way to walking to the end of the neighborhood. I was going to start it today but it's way too cold outside and I'm sore from the walking around I did yesterday. So, after I take Peanut to daycare tomorrow, I might go to the park and walk before I have to get my testing done at work. I have to remember to start slow. Every time I say I'm going to start walking, I overdo it on the first go and then spend the rest of the day in pain.

Alright, back to writing. I'll worry about my need for exercise later.

Thursday, March 31, 2022

I had a surprisingly productive day today, despite having some sniffles. (Allergies, gotta love it) I got up early this morning and did some revisions on what I have so far for Plot Bunny. I'm almost done with chapter 4! And then it was time to wake Peanut.

We played and watched Mythbuster reruns. She colored for a bit. So, I know I have to start rotating her artwork on the dining room walls. We're running out of space!

When I laid her down for Quiet Time, I did my semi-regular gaming livestream. That's always a lot of fun. I've been playing this farming simulation game called Stardew Valley. I managed to play about a week game time in the 2(ish) hours of the video.

When that was over, I joined my friends KL and GF for their livestream. I decided to have a big planning session. It's the last day of the month. I have 3 projects I want to release to the world in the coming months. I need to have a plan in place. I also know that having some flexibility is key in case life happens and deadlines need to be moved. So, I wrote my goals on little sticky notes and put them in my planner.

Along with the publishing, I really want to reach Affiliate status on Twitch. Then, my channel will be monetized! So, I'm trying to get back on a good schedule and I'm reaching out to people to restart my Creator Spotlight series. I have a huge file loaded with questions to ask and names of people I want to talk with. This will require reaching out which is prompting the Anxiety Brain, because of course it is. But, I had a lot of fun with this series last year. They were some of my most watched videos.

Oh! And, I'm going to be a guest on a podcast! By the time you are reading this, it'll likely be out. But, CE asked me to record an episode with them about the Gilded Age show that we are both obsessed with. Their show is called Project: Shadow. The first season of Gilded Age just concluded and oh my GOSH it was SO GOOD! I haven't been so excited about a television show since I first got into Doctor Who nearly a decade ago. Before that, my show of choice was Buffy. I would literally drop whatever I was in the middle of at 9:00 to go watch it. And, CE's podcast does a lot of pop culture chat so this topic fits right in.

I'm excited and nervous. Of course, I want to gush about this show. And, it's a good way to promote to potential new readers. But, Anxiety Brain has to be a jerk and come up with all the ways I'll mess it up. So, I have to constantly tell it to shut up and let me do the think. "Silence the Imp" as MM says. New experiences are good! And, it's also networking and marketing for my work. This is the year of publishing after all. My goal is three projects, like I said. It's insane but I am determined to pull it off. No more delays. No more excuses.

What are those three projects, you ask? Well, the first one I've wanted to get out for many years. It's my contemporary fantasy that I've been referring to just as "Witches." I'm shooting for a fall release. The developmental edits went great. I need to schedule line edits. Also, going to work with CE and see if they can help with a cover and formatting. I have a mockup of an ebook cover but it needs work. I have an image that I want on the cover. Beyond that, uh…

Project 2 is Plot Bunny. That will be serialized. Writing it is my goal for April and I'm shooting for sometime later in spring to have it up on Vella. I'm enjoying everything about this story and the world I've been creating for it. It's a nice reality escape.

Project 3 is this project that has so far been in serial form but I'm doing a compiled release of the first 50 entries. I'm hoping to have a release in August, on my dad's birthday. I'll be reaching out to local bookstores to do events if they allow them yet and there is an arts fest in the town I grew up in that I might get a table at.

The first quarter of 2022 was a rough start for a lot of reasons. So, I'm treating quarter 2 as a kind of reboot. I'm doing Camp NaNoWriMo with my friends. Weather is improving so more chances to take Peanut on little adventures. I'll be able to book the hotel for the September trip soon. Things are looking up!

Saturday, April 2, 2022

So... last night I revised a few of the chapters for Plot Bunny that I have already written and I started scheduling them to go up on Vella in May near Peanut's birthday. Am I insane? Probably. But, I could not wait any more. And, I figured it's incentive to keep working on it. If people are reading it, they are going to want a complete story. So, I have the prologue and chapter 1-4 scheduled to go. I feel like I am back in my fan fiction days, posting a little at a time. Except now it's part of my job. How cool is that!

I know I have been talking a lot about it but it's become something I really look forward to working on each day. It's got some wild parts that I can't wait to write and share with everyone. And, the ideas I have already been brainstorming for book 2 just make me all giddy.

Also, the world I've been creating is so much fun. It's a blend of different cultures and creatures. There are different kinds of magic users and a massive pantheon. It's definitely my escape from the real world and I hope it can be for others as well in some way.

I am also excited for July. I am planning on participating in World Anvil Summer Camp again so I can write up all the world building information in my giant binder. I would make certain things available for public view. (I think they have to be public to be counted toward the prompts) And the prompts can help me come up with things I hadn't maybe thought of before. I might do better than last year. It was a challenge trying to apply fantasy prompts to a real world-like setting.

I don't know how much writing I will get done this weekend. Work weekends are difficult in the productivity category. But, I have big plans for the coming weeks. I want to hit at least half way this week on Plot Bunny and spend the weekends on revisions and coming up with titles. Once Plot Bunny is done and launched, I plan on spending all of May back on "Witches" to get it out in August. I want it available in case I am free to do the arts fest in the town I grew up in. As long as it's not the same weekend Bestie and I are going on our Renaissance Fair trip. I emailed the people in charge of the festival asking them to let me know when they have a date. I also plan on emailing a couple bookstores about carrying my work. There are two prominent ones not too far from me I would love to work with!

In 2023, I want to start attending more conferences and conventions. I know CE used to go to a lot of conventions. Maybe we could get a table together and split the cost. Those events can get expensive. Table fees, having a stock of books, travel costs, promo material and all that. But, it's an excuse to travel!

Having all these plans is helping me stay productive. It could be the Plague and all the restrictions still in place causing the cabin fever to kick in. Or, the fact that I've been wanting to publish for nearly a decade and I'm tired of thinking about it. Let's get it done and do all the things!

I brought out my official "Hold My Purse 2022" notebook and I've been writing down ideas of events I want to look into after I get "Witches" out into the wider world. The local library system does have an Indie Author conference in the fall and there is a huge book sale so I submitted my contact info for that. I'm going to email the bookstores about hosting a launch event, maybe working with the library? Since the Writers Center has helped me so much, I'd like to include them. I also want to see how I can submit a copy of my books to be on library shelves. So many things to consider!

I better get working on more of those things.

Friday, April 15, 2022

We are halfway through the month and my draft of Plot Bunny is nearly done! I've started revising and fleshing out details as I complete each chapter and then it gets scheduled for Vella! I'll have another story out in the world! I have the launch set for early May near Peanut's birthday so it's easy to remember and then each following episode will drop on Thursdays. Once I am done with all of that, it is back to the modern world as I jump back into "Witches." The plan is to do one more read-through and schedule line edits in May.

Next on my list is formatting and cover. I have an image that I want on the cover and I managed to make it in the mock-up I made. I know I will need help formatting my document. I spent 2 hours in Word fighting with a pre-made document. No matter how I spaced things and resized the font. I ended up with multiple pages where just a single final line of a chapter was there and it drove me crazy. So I need to enlist help from someone a bit more skilled than I am and, maybe, with better software.

I am so excited to have both of these stories out in the world. "Witches" has been a labor of love for 8 years now, which is just insane to me. And, it's not just one book. I have 4 in varying stages of complete from first draft to ready for developmental edits. Given all the changes I made to book 1 after those edits, I will me making many more adjustments to the next 3 and beyond.

The character of Tara has been in my head long before I wrote "Witches." Towards the end of high school, into my community college days, I would do online roleplay with friends. Not with dice rolls or anything like a tabletop game. But, on forums and instant messenger group chats. We would take on a character and write part of a story from their perspective. Many late nights fueled by Mountain Dew and candy coming up with wild stories about an evil Cookie Monster or the one time there was a spell and everyone ended up in the bodies of characters of popular TV shows and movies. (We had a goth Pink Ranger at one point, I kid you not.)

As I started working on "Witches," there was no question this was Tara's origin story and it evolved from there. I have ideas for almost 10 books at least. I have notebooks loaded with prompts and ideas.

The one thing about a character being in your head for nearly 20 years is she is so easy to write! That made book 3 harder to write because I shifted point of view to another character for that story. It took me 3 years at least to get into the head of this other person, even though she is in the whole series. She's just not the primary view. But, I wanted a perspective from a character who has always been a witch and has always lived in the small town where the story is set so we get to know her and her life.

I also had to fight the urge to start brainstorming a prequel series. Tara's grandmother, Caitlin, is a character I fell in love with right away. And, her story could be so fascinating if I took the time to fill in the details. At the start of book 1, she's in her mid 80s. She had her final child when she was over 50! She's sassy and brilliant and a mixture of both my grandmothers and my dad and several other people I've known throughout my life. Maybe one day I'll get that prequel series but I want to finish my initial series first. And, the first book will be available soon! It's a dream come true.

And I can't believe my little Peanut is going to be 3 in just a couple short weeks! We have a follow-up meeting this week about her evaluation for preschool so we can start registering her for the next school year. And, yes, I will absolutely be that mom who bursts into tears after dropping her off on the first day of school. Especially if she acts like she does for daycare. A blown kiss and a wave goodbye and off she goes! I got a little choked up the first time that happened. She's my only baby and she's growing up.

And, you're probably reading this and rolling your eyes. Like, "Carey, come on. Yes, kids will grow up. It's a part of life." Yes, I am aware of this. But, it is a different feeling I can't really explain. As much as I could trade in the tantrums and the stubbornness (because, yes, she is my child in that regard for sure. I'm admitting it in print! Dad would be pleased), seeing how far she's come from where she started so small has been astounding to me. I tell everyone she's my miracle baby because she is.

I can only hope she takes that fire in her and learns to channel it toward good things. Maybe she'll start a foundation or work for some sort of social justice cause. Maybe she'll be a nurse and care for other preemies. Or, she'll be a pop star. The way she dances and tries to sing in the car is fantastic. We have a mother-daughter karaoke session on our drives to appointments or wherever we have to go and it's a blast. I can't wait for the weather to be warmer and I have the car windows down so the world can hear us not have a care in the world as we sing our hearts out.

Anyway, back to work. I have books to release. Ah!!

Tuesday, April 26, 2022

Just over a week until "Adventures in Thira" goes live to… well, the US if you're reading through Vella. I have to get it up on my crowdfunding platform still for the rest of the world to read. But, still! I'm publishing! And, yes, I finally figured out a title. "Adventures in Thira," formerly known as the Plot Bunny. I still might use that nickname just because it's become stuck in my head, at least for a little while.

I am so excited to share this story! I want to know what people think about it. It gets ridiculous at some points. I have a few hammy bits, like the villain bent on vengeance and world domination. There are fantasy creatures and magic. And, this is just the first book. It's a glimpse at the world I've been building these past few months. I've been working on ideas for book 2 that takes place in the capital city of Thira, the country my story is set in. I'm not sure how long it will take to nail down and finish but I'm giving a general goal of early 2023. I can move that goal post to earlier as I am able to. If things go as planned, I could have a draft done for July

Camp NaNoWriMo. But, I have a lot of other things to do to prep for the release of "Witches" at the end of the summer. I started a read through and making notes over the weekend and I'm getting pretty hyped for the release!

I've had to change up my routine a bit. I went to the doctor last week and I am diabetic. The doctor wants me to try for a few months to see if I can manage with just diet and exercise. So, I've cut the soda pop. I've tried getting healthier snacks-crackers, cucumbers, hard boiled eggs, cheese, thinks like that. As the weather gets warmer, more fresh fruit will be available for smoothies and treats like that. Every time I go grocery shopping, I'm looking out for fresh watermelon. It should be coming out soon! I've been trying to do this for a while. This diagnosis is the kick in the pants I probably will need to take it more seriously.

Hotel for the ren fair is booked! It's official! Soon we'll get our tickets and it's a matter of saving up spending money and getting accessories for my costumes. I have one gown that I will probably wear that Saturday. And then there's one I told Hubby I want for my birthday for day 2. I've also been eying some items on Etsy to complete the look. I also started another crochet project. I made a cloak earlier in the year, complete with a hood. It came out so nice. And now I'm just making a long shawl. It won't take too long to make. I can probably bust it out in a few weeks as long as my wrists hold out. I did make it really long, though. It takes an hour to do one row. So, my max progress will be one maybe 2 per day just so my hands don't cramp up.

We're also planning birthday celebrations for the Peanut! Actually on her birthday, we'll have my mom and in-laws over for dinner. And then a few weeks after, we'll do a little party with my sister and maybe some aunts and uncles. May is a hit-or-miss when it comes to weather in the Great Lakes region. As a May baby myself, there were many birthday parties held in June when sunshine and warmer temperatures were a bit more guaranteed. It'll be fun, though. If my sister and Bestie are free to join us for the second party, all the kids can run around together. We don't have a very big yard but we can break out the sidewalk chalk and the bubbles and they'll have a blast, I'm sure. And, I'll feel a little better now that our sidewalk has been fixed.

The next few months are going to be crazy with all the release stuff for these stories, and birthday stuff, and getting ready for the ren fair. Also, I am determined to take Peanut on adventures this summer. Like back to the zoo. She's never been to the beach. There is an event in the town I grew up in where they have a band every week in the town square throughout the summer. I know Peanut will love that because all things music! I'll be trying to coordinate with my mom and my sister to include them, too. It's always a challenge coordinating schedules but I think we can figure something out.

I keep referring to my Hold My Purse theme for the year. Time to do all the things!

Thursday, May 5, 2022

It's release day! "Adventures in Thira" book 1 has started to release on Vella! I have the prologue and chapters 1 and 2 ready and up. I'm so excited!! They officially went live today and I got up super early to spam the web with the links. (I'm technically taking the day off for family stuff but I had to promote this.) And then the rest of it will come out on Thursdays a chapter at a time. I hope people like this story. I really do. I've had so much fun writing it and building the world.

I think in July I'm going to do World Building summer camp in addition to starting book 2. Then I can share the world with everyone. I have 2 massive binders full of stuff that I have been working on for months and the prompts will help come up with more ideas. I'm still working on the Pantheon Binder. There are a LOT of deities in this world... and that may change because it's a bit overwhelming. So, I might have to combine a few to shrink it down.

So, what am I going to do to celebrate this occasion? Well, today is the day we're having family over for Peanut's birthday so I'll be working on prepping dinner and tidying the house. This weekend is Mother's Day. I already treated myself to a couple little accessories for my costume for the ren fair trip. I found a cute little cloak clasp, a necklace, and a pouch to loop onto my belt. That might be the extent of my shopping so I have spending money for the trip itself. For my birthday, I asked Hubby for another dress and a new pair of shoes. My tennis shoes have seen better days. I got them before I got married and they're not as comfortable as they used to be. I saw a really nice looking pair on one of my favorite clothing sites so I may order those as a dual release/birthday present. They look comfortable and the ratings say they're good for a lot of walking, which will come in handy this summer.

I also think I might go out for a nice dinner as well. Get some friends together and get dressed up. It's a matter of seeing who's comfortable with going to a restaurant. If it's warm enough, we could do outdoor seating and maybe more people will be willing to take part.

With my planned adventures, I have an idea for some vlogs on my YouTube channel. I try and highlight the area I live in as much as I can. The Cleveland area is beautiful but we're kind of looked down upon by other areas of the country. Even earning the nickname "Mistake on the Lake." So, a lot of locals try to battle that reputation. Sure, we've had a rough past. Sure, our river caught on fire... more than once... but we're getting better. So, when I take Peanut on our little field trips, I want to try and vlog about it and show off all the wonderful things in my area. I have 2 videos just on the zoo. I'd love to feature the parks and museums. There's an International Garden. We may even try to go to a baseball game. (Not sure we'll take Peanut for that. She's a bit too young and the sensory overload will be a bit much. May make it a date night.) I'd like to get a new camera. The one I have is big and awkward and is at least 12 years old so could die any day. It takes great pictures, still. And, it's my camera for sit down discussion videos. I'd like something a little more compact for out and about that I can toss in my purse and now worry about busting. But, a new camera is expensive and not in the cards this year. Instead, I will get a MicroSD card for my phone and use that for the time being.

Time to go get ready for family time. And I will try to resist obsessively checking social media and my stats to see if anyone's read the chapters that are up.

Volume 1 Conclusion

WRITTEN: MAY 6, 2022

Well, here we are. This concludes volume 1! Yes, this is just the first of many I hope to write about this journey I'm on of author-parent-whatever life. There are many more adventures ahead that I can't wait to share with you all. But, I'm trying to stick to a certain amount of entries to get this out in a regular set of time. And, now that I have that first fiction story out in the world, I encourage you to go read it, if you enjoy fantasy.

If you have something creative you want to do, whether that is painting, writing, making jewelry, starting a podcast, do it! It won't be easy. Especially if you're juggling parenting, a job, caring for a loved one. So, it doesn't have to be a career. Just an enjoyable hobby. That's how I started out. With just a love of telling stories. And, that love grew as I learned and developed and it was possible to pursue it as a career. It's a juggling act and it helps that I have a support system behind me. Not everyone has that. But, try to do it anyway. Don't let others take away what makes you happy. There is so much going on in the world that isn't good. We need to find those joys in life to make it worth getting up in the morning. Even if it's only in a few spare moments a day, a week, a month.

So, what's ahead in volume 2 and beyond? At the time I'm writing this, Adventurers of Thira has been out for a whole day. I'm still making minor tweaks as I schedule each chapter so that's one task for the rest of the month. Also, the edits for "Welcome to Coolersville," the first book in the contemporary fantasy series, continues before I send that off to be professionally line edited. That will come out this summer, I'm thinking later August.

When I get all these things out, I'm hoping to get more information on an Indie Author conference that's held through the library sometime in the fall. I sent in my contact info letting them know I was interested in having a table at the book sale. This is a big step and, after I filled out the form, I had a moment of, "Oh, crap. What did I just do? Pressure's on now to keep to my deadlines."

Then, there's all the excitement happening with Peanut. Another summer of new adventures. This year we'll be able to see family more as things start to (hopefully, maybe, please, God) improve with the Plague. So, you know I'll be texting my mom and sister and planning things for the kiddos to do. I want to take Peanut to the zoo, the beach (I haven't been to the beach in 4 years, guys. I'm dying a little), all the museums we have around town. And then there's getting her ready for preschool! What?! My baby girl is a school kid now! We started the registration last week and I got her physical forms filled out by the doctor.

I encourage you to reach out to me on social media and share whatever you're working on. I'm CareyHAuthor on nearly everything. You can get updates on all I'm doing. I don't always respond to direct messages and I screen comments to avoid spam and trolling but I do my best with everything else.

Thanks for reading! Your support means the world to me. And, I look forward to sharing my continuing journey with you and all the misadventures that come along with it.

Made in the USA
Middletown, DE
17 November 2022